Adva
The G

Jay Michaelson's incisive and exquisitely profound insights into our human condition come in full force in THE GATE OF TEARS. A *Pensées* for our time, THE GATE OF TEARS offers deep thinking about our lives that gets us thinking – and feeling. Here we have an antidote to the mindless feel-good ideology, and gentle instructions in attending to the fullness of our experience so we see the value in the downs, not just the ups. Our inner world will never seem the same.

Daniel Goleman, author of *Emotional Intelligence* and *A Force for Good: The Dalai Lama's Vision for Our World*

Jay Michaelson's best book yet is accessible, inviting, and written like poetry. Seamlessly blending teachings from Buddhist, Jewish, and humanistic traditions, THE GATE OF TEARS will be of enormous help to anyone hiding or fighting any part of themselves.

Sylvia Boorstein, author of *Happiness is an Inside Job*

THE GATE OF TEARS is a beautifully written, transformative book. Jay Michaelson guides us, instead of denying, avoiding, explaining away or resisting sadness, to go right into the heart of it. There we find open space, true love of life, and, perhaps most redeeming, one another.

Sharon Salzberg, author of *Lovingkindness* and *Real Happiness*

There are two kinds of mystics: those who talk about the mystical and those who speak from and for it. Jay Michaelson is among the latter. THE GATE OF TEARS is an invitation to authentic mystical awakening offered by a seeker who dares to be crushed by God that he might be freed for godliness. Don't just read this book; digest it.

Rabbi Rami Shapiro, author of *Perennial Wisdom for the Spiritually Independent*

Sometimes with a Jewish eye, sometimes with a Buddhist eye, but always keenly focused on wisdom, Jay Michaelson teaches us to distinguish sorrow from despair and sadness from depression. Surely the entrance to the gate of tears is familiar to us all, but his gift here is to walk us through the gate and lead us into a territory full of the promise of healing and redemption. A rabbi, a scholar, a poet, and a leader, Michaelson is a learned but personable and personal guide, and by showing us how he has learned to be kind to himself, he teaches us how to be kind to others.

Rodger Kamenetz, author of *The Jew in the Lotus*, and *Burnt Books: Rabbi Nachman of Bratzlav and Franz Kafka*.

Jay Michaelson's exquisitely rendered THE GATE OF TEARS offers the evocative reflections of a soul who knows firsthand the poignant pain of deep sorrow, loneliness, and loss, yet poetically presents a view that includes these difficult aspects of the human condition. He illuminates a contemplative perspective that allows for the full symphony of one's life and spiritual journey, within which sadness is but a lyrical melody in a minor key. His words can soothe and heal the broken heart.

Eliezer Sobel, author of *Minyan: Ten Jewish Men in a World that is Heartbroken*

A stunning antidote to the plethora of "get happy" guides, Jay Michaelson reminds us that sadness is as necessary a part of the human condition as joy, and that in embracing both, we experience what it is to be fully alive. Inspired by religion, poetry, and Michaelson's honest reflections, THE GATE OF TEARS is a book that, in embracing sadness, celebrates life.

Rabbi Dan Ain, Director of Tradition and Innovation at 92nd St. Y.

The Gate of Tears
Sadness and the Spiritual Path

Jay Michaelson

Foreword by Lama Surya Das

Ben Yehuda Press
Teaneck, New Jersey

ISBN13: 978-1-934730-45-4

Library of Congress Cataloging-in-Publication Data

Michaelson, Jay, 1971- author.
 The gate of tears : sadness and the spiritual path / Jay Michaelson; foreword by Lama Surya Das.
    pages cm
 Includes bibliographical references.
 ISBN 978-1-934730-45-4
 1. Spirituality. 2. Spiritual life. 3. Sadness--Religious aspects. 4. Suffering--Religious life. I. Title.
  BL624.M4736 2015
  204'.42--dc23

                                      2015036087

"Luck" from THE COLLECTED POEMS OF LANGSTON HUGHES by Langston Hughes, edited by Arnold Rampersad with David Roessel, Associate Editor, copyright © 1994 by the Estate of Langston Hughes. Used by permission of Alfred A. Knopf, an imprint of the Knopf Doubleday Publishing Group, a division of Penguin Random House LLC. All rights reserved.

Also by Jay Michaelson

God in Your Body: Kabbalah, Mindfulness, and Embodied
    Spiritual Practice
Everything is God: The Radical Path of Nondual Judaism
Another Word for Sky: Poems
God vs. Gay? The Religious Case for Equality
Redefining Religious Liberty: The Covert Campaign Against
    Civil Rights
Evolving Dharma: Meditation, Buddhism, and the Next
    Generation of Enlightenment

Sometimes a crumb falls
from the tables of joy
Sometimes a bone
is flung.

To some people
love is given,
To others,
only heaven.

—Langston Hughes, "Luck"

Even though the gates of prayer are closed,
the gates of tears are open.

—Talmud Berachot 32b

The Gate of Tears

Contents

The Gate of Tears

Foreword

by Lama Surya Das

When I'm asked to write a foreword, I'm not sure whether to toast or roast the writer. In this case it's more clear. My dear friend Jay has written about roasting in the flames of suffering, so no need for me to fan them. But the good news is that Jay's found a way to co-meditate with them, rather than trying to run from or avoid them, as so many of us often wish to do. As he himself said to me, "Instead of self-help, this book is self-help-less. Surrender to sadness and it mingles with joy."

Here we have a wonderful contemplation on what it means to be human, to suffer the pains and losses inevitable in life as we know it. I myself have had to learn the hard way that a few tears can water the spiritual garden, while reams of wise words from nonprofit prophets simply won't. Early on I heard from my late grandfather that life ain't easy, and that God ain't found on the mountaintops but in the ashes. My grandfather was Jewish, however, and from Russia, so I thought I didn't have to accept that assessment. But he was right.

Rabbi Dr. Jay M, our author-scout on the frontier of consciousness, reports back to us that he set out to meditate and find God, truth and wisdom, and found only himself. Although I would take this with a grain of salt, I get the gist. This may be the bad news and the good news, all in one. Momentous decisions, conclusions, epiphanies, breakthroughs and breakdowns too, often come in paroxysms as we grow up, evolve, age and die, and continue in the greater ecology of being.

Finding himself in a dark wood in mid-life, along with Dante, and seeing through a glass darkly—including losing his mother amidst the process of bringing this book to life—Jay has provided himself and us both with a portal into the depths and heights of our shared human experience. He invites us to feel the feelings he feels and empathize with him in our shared human condition. This painful yet productive internal journey has made him even more of a *mensch* and a bodhisattva, permeable to and empathic with the sufferings and travails of the world. I love and respect him even more than usual for that inner fortitude, faith, and resilience. He inspires a skeptical sod like me, and that ain't easy! For who doesn't suffer from loss, change, disappointment, existential angst, and daily stress amidst "the slings and arrows of outrageous fortune"? Not *moi*.

The Buddhist virtue known as equanimity (*upeksha*), calm and clear, is fine as far as it goes. Yet when it comes to grief and the tragedies of life, even the legendary Tibetan master Marpa the Translator cried and caterwauled for three days when his teenage son Dharma Dode was thrown from a horse, cracked his head on a rock, and died, one thousand years ago. And when an old couple who had been his students came and respectfully asked Marpa why he was weeping and wailing so bitterly, since he'd always taught that life is impermanent, tenuous, hollow, ephemeral and insubstantial, like a dream, the master himself exclaimed: "Yes, but the death of a child is like a super-dream, a real nightmare!" Then he threw his maroon lama-robe over his head and keened loudly for a few more days.

I find this Tibetan teaching tale quite instructive. We can talk all we want about nonattachment and emptiness, but what

I lovingly call the glorious *neurotic-kaya* also has its place—the dark-side or challenging messiness of emotionality, confusion and hangups, and the wisdom side of the emotions co-emergent with them. Let us remember the ancient dictum that shadows are nothing but light. Thus neuroses are also the clear light of reality, as Mahamudra masters might say. We overlook this innate natural resource at our peril.

Feeling can be healing, especially for those of us brought up and conditioned to suppress and repress difficult feelings and emotions, dark moods and painful memories, perhaps compensating with habitual behaviors not always in our best interests. How does it work? As Jay explains, by bringing alert present awareness to mindfully feeling our feelings, as they arise, and letting them come and go with space and awareness, leaving room for healthy experience of them and integration, in their own time and place. Embracing intense inner emotions with nonreactive, open, friendly and even curious presence of mind, and with complete acceptance of whatever momentarily arises in the body-mind continuum, without judgment or evaluation. I find this extraordinarily helpful.

Years ago, I sat like a teenage Buddha statue, meditating for long hours in gardens and woods, caves, deserts and on foreign mountainsides. How amazed I was to discover that a gritty black coal mine makes one as rich as a diamond one. What an awakening this was, and is! Black is the new lustre. And to discover that letting go actually means letting come and go, letting be, leading to vast relief, self-acceptance, inner peace and equanimity… *quelle surprise*! There is nirvanic peace in things left just as they are. Emaho!

Shadows are nothing but light, friends and seekers. Tears can wash away the dust covering one's inner eye, clarifying things as if for the first time. We come to see things differently and not just see different things. The ancient Pearl Principle I made up a few books back tells us that without an inner irritant, no pearl gets produced in the fertile inner darkness of the soul. This is precisely how we can gain through loss, and uncover the authentic virtue of adversity.

In this book, we find a real human being seeking real truth, clarity, meaningful connection and love. This candid and introspective first-person reflection is a royal road to riches, and to that wisdom and wealth of contentment that the sages throughout the ages all extol as if with one voice. Read it and weep, laugh, start a journal yourself. Or stand up, raise your gaze, open your arms, and breathe. I'm about to break into song, so better end here. Better yet, let's together sing the words of Rabbi Cohen, that there's a crack in everything, and that's where the light gets in. Or where it already is.

Lama Surya Das
Dzogchen Center
Cambridge, MA
April 2015

Introduction

Joy and sadness are not opposites. Sometimes, they coexist, like two consonant notes of a complex yet harmonious chord. Many spiritual paths begin with the awareness of suffering. The Buddha leaves his comfortable life when he first encounters old age, sickness, and death outside the palace walls. The Children of Israel come of age only after centuries of slavery—and with ancestors said to have wandered, struggled, and mourned. Christ in the wilderness and on the cross, Arjuna on the battlefield. And although spirituality today is alleged by its critics to be narcissistic and escapist, anyone who takes contemplative practice seriously finds instead an uncovering of that which was hidden—and as a consequence, a confrontation with pain.

Ironically, religion is quite often the opposite. Religion often promises the erasure of sadness, perhaps in some future world after death, or perhaps in a life of everlasting joy lived in the light of God. Perhaps the shift is sudden, in a moment of enlightenment, or perhaps gradual, as one banishes sadness through ardency, or prayer, or by "manifesting" a world in which lack no longer exists. Or perhaps the spaces in between are filled by the 'knowledge' that one is special, chosen, immortal, saved, or destined.

In these instances, what begins with suffering leads to its supposed erasure. So we are told.

This is not the case only among the religious. At our contemporary moment, the ordinary sadness that is part of a life richly lived is often stigmatized, shamed, deemed a kind of American failure. In our hyper-capitalist and fast-moving popular culture, sadness is a secularized sin; America is about the pursuit of happiness, after all—so start pursuing. Eliminate sadness with entertainment, bury it with goods, do whatever it takes to forget it. Melancholy, once regarded as a sign of sensitivity, is sometimes mistaken to be a symptom of depression, thus trivializing both. And serious people, we are told, don't do spirituality.

Neither the spiritual nor the material repression of sadness reflects the depth of contemplative life. The great irony is that the very effort to feel joy (or relief) prevents its fruition. Perhaps counterintuitively, it is the surrender to sadness that causes it to pass—not the suppression of it. The gestures of opening, making-space, giving-way—these enable a delicious relinquishment, a setting down of the burden, even, perhaps, a kind of wisdom.

Contemplative practice does bring about a deep, abiding joy. Yet this "simple feeling of being," as one teacher describes it, co-exists quite beautifully with sadness, merges with it like notes in a minor chord. The deep joy of awakening is a happiness not of merriment or exuberance, but a love that reveals itself precisely when sadness or other difficult emotions are allowed to unfold just as they are. It is a joy of relinquishing, allowing, setting down the burden. The spiritual search, then, is really the cessation of searching. No more manipulating experience in order to feel better (what will it be *this* time?), no more lurching out of the mind for satisfaction. But letting go, letting be, and giving up.

This is counterintuitive wisdom, I think, yet it is at the heart of the world's great contemplative traditions—certainly the ones I have spent time exploring. It is at the core of the Buddha's teaching that grasping, pushing away, and ignorance are the roots of suffering. It resonates in the liturgy of my Jewish tradition, in the poetry of its psalms and in the biographies of its flawed and redemptive heroes. And it is present in countless artistic expressions. Darkness and light are interwoven, interdependent; God brings forth both sun and shade.

This is what I understand as the gate of tears, through which one finds insight, liberation, even mysticism. The art of being with sadness, and other unwanted houseguests of the mind, brings about an intimacy with what is—what the mystics call the One, the Divine, the Beloved. Crying out in sadness is an expression of holiness and of art. And the tone of sadness is, itself, beautiful in its way.

Such tones of heart may be occasioned by life-changing events, such as the death of a loved one or other significant loss. Like all of us, I have experienced these passages, and I have written this book in the shadow of one of them. But my primary focus here is what might be called "ordinary sadness," part of the oscillations of mood which are part of any life lived deliberately. Loneliness arises, and doubt, and occasional regret; this is not symptomatic of pathology but part of the ebb and flow of the human experience.

Still, the gate of tears is the less chosen way. Among my high-functioning colleagues in the worlds of journalism and advocacy, it seems like a kind of weakness. And among the religious, contemplative traditions are generally minority expressions of spiritual life; more popular ones, rightly occupied with providing comfort for those who need it, have a hundred compensatory myths. We are chosen, we are part of the Divine dance, we are saved, we are at the End Times, we are fulfilling the destiny of the human race. Such teachings doubtless provide comfort, which is what they seem designed to do. But they are often self-defeating. If I am part of the Divine dance, why do I still feel unhappy? If I'm so spiritual, what am I doing wrong? If religion provides a sense of communal purpose, then it is precisely this sense of discontinuity, displacement, and disunity that births the spiritual path.

*　*　*

I went on my first meditation retreat, years ago, with the intention of achieving enlightenment. Not right away, of course, but hopefully, eventually. Along the way, I thought that I might have some of the wonderful, transformative experiences that I'd read and written about as a scholar of religion. (In addition to my rabbinic ordination and Buddhist teaching lineage, I have a Ph.D. in Jewish Thought, and have studied and taught religion in academic contexts for twenty years.) So I went on that first retreat, ready to see God.

Instead, I saw myself. To my dismay, I found great loneliness, emotional scars from fifteen years of hiding and denying my sexuality, and, above all, a bundle of tactics to avoid seeing clearly—the way I was seeing now, it seemed, for the first time. This wasn't what I had signed up for. I was on retreat for *devekut*, for *samadhi*, for visions and mind-states and unions and attainments—not *therapy*. And anyway, I was supposed to be "above" all that. I had been a successful software entrepreneur, a Yale-educated lawyer, and was now making my way as an LGBT activist and supposedly hard-edged journalist. What was I doing with—gasp—my "inner child"?

Eventually, some of those visions and ecstasies did arrive—and pass, as they inevitably do—and I have been blessed with many years of powerful and profound experiences, far beyond anything I would have imagined on that first retreat. But over time, these experiences became a kind of sideshow. In fact, the so-called "therapy" was the real work. On retreat after retreat, I confronted, wrestled with, and finally allowed myself to be defeated by, the sadness and loneliness that would often arise when the chatter of my mind subsided.

Gradually, I learned to create a kind of internal spaciousness around self-doubt, self-hatred, and pain. And as I made room for the shadows, my eyes got used to the dark. I became intimate with the internal geographies of my heart. I progressed along the contemplative path as described in the Theravadan Buddhist tradition, while also maintaining a Jewish devotional practice, both of which I have written about elsewhere. I found that liberation does arise; it is possible to uncover a simple joy of being itself—a joy that has no opposite. And I have written this book because, over time, I have found a reservoir of deep joy precisely in the moments of occasional sadness that attend all who choose to live life sensitive to its movements and momentums. If earlier in my spiritual path I saw these difficult encounters as unfortunate but necessary stops along the way, eventually I came to see them as the way itself.

I am not a doctor, and this is not a book about depression, or any other medical condition. I am not qualified to offer any medical advice, and do not pretend to do so. However, as someone who has experienced depression at times in my life, I feel qualified to say that sadness is not the same thing. Depression is a medical condition, a function of brain chemistry. It can be crippling, devastating, bleak. It makes it hard to live one's life. Subjectively, I experienced it as a dullness, a kind of lessening, or graying, of all emotion. Sadness, on the other hand, is part of being human. So is loss, pain, and loneliness. These are not veils in the way of feeling; they *are* feeling. They have their own hues and characters. Unlike depression, sadness does not worsen when one yields to it; it softens, teaches, makes way. And in the yielding is some of the quality of liberation itself.

As I have already said, this sort of ordinary sadness need not come about under special circumstances. I have been revising the manuscript of this book during the *shloshim* period, the thirty days of intensive mourning, after the death of my mother. I wrote its first draft many years ago, when I was still emerging from the 'closet' and despairing of ever finding love. In the years since, I have met with children disowned by the parents and with children whose parents died suddenly; with men who had struggled with loneliness their whole lives and with men who lost lovers to AIDS. I have found the wisdom I relate here to be of some use at extreme times such as these. But the primary orientation of this book is toward circumstances altogether more ordinary: it is about the everyday blues, melancholy—enlightenment in a minor key.

In a similar vein, I often, as part of my work, give talks on abstruse subjects ranging from constitutional law to Kabbalah, gender theory to geoengineering. I am a quasi-academic, and love the life of the mind; I can quote Levinas and Lou Reed, Nathan of Gaza and Michel Foucault. But while there are plenty of books with esoteric wisdom, the Secret, the Answer, or the Way, this is not one of them. On the contrary, in my experience, the way to deep and profound joy, to a radiant love of life, is precisely by not expecting any answer—not expecting experience to be any particular way.

To find the answer is not the answer. Not-knowing is more powerful than knowing, simple vulnerability more resonant than the baroque convolutions of esoterica or the tired poses of cynics. Most of my profound insights seem banal when written; the liberation is in the seeing. So, although there is a kind of secret here, this path is not an esoteric one. It is not a cure for sadness. It is more self-helpless than self-help. And it is not an encyclopedia of wisdom or pithy quotes. In my view, these tactics dispel precisely those movements of mind which should be accepted, held, and relinquished only with the gentlest release.

Finally, I have chosen to write this book in first-person language, because I know of no way to express the truths I want to tell except in terms of how I have experienced them. It comes with my privilege, my perspective, my gender, my spiritual paths. I focus on Dharma, humanism, and Judaism not because they are superior paths, but because they are the ones I have followed the furthest. And although I am writing this book more in my role as meditation teacher and rabbi, it is also informed by my training as a scholar and my work (and sensibility) as a writer, commentator, lawyer—and skeptic in, I hope, the best sense of the word. There is no pretense of universality here.

Occasionally, particularly in Part Three, I use the word "God." I apologize to those alienated and wounded by this term—your rejection of it is more than justified. I also apologize to those who hold dear to a certain meaning of it, since the way I use it is different from how many (most?) religious people do. To me, God is a name that humans give to all that is. Experientially, it is whatever is left over when the delusion of the self is taken away. For example, in programs of recovery, the essential movement of "let God hold that burden" is not a particular theology, but rather "let me not try to do so." This, to me, is the confluence of my theistic and non-theistic spiritual paths: the relinquishment of the natural yet wrong notion that the separate self between my ears is the arbiter of reality. I am not interested in ontological discussions of God, but I am enriched by experiential encounters with a love that seems to transcend our finitude. This experience is the result of a choice, a personalization of everything and nothing. Is it merely a projection of the mind? Maybe it is. Yet I have found this mode of purported relationship to awaken both wisdom and compassion. So I'll keep using it, and keep apologizing for using it.

*   *   *

Part One of *The Gate of Tears* describes what I have called here a counter-intuitive kind of contemplative practice: yielding to, rather than banishing, sadness. Surprisingly (at least to me), this yielding—rather than explaining, justifying, escaping, denying, or seeking to erase—is itself a movement of liberation. This attitude toward the unpleasant is derived primarily from the Dharma; it is a particular expression the Buddha's four noble truths, which propose that freedom is less a matter of changing the conditions of our lives than changing the way in which we relate to those conditions. It combines some aspects of Theravadan training, particularly insight meditation, with some of the Tantric aspects (in the original sense) of Tibetan Buddhism. The Buddha, it is sometimes forgotten, was called by his contemporaries "The Happy One." Not the dour one, or the detached one—but profoundly, abidingly happy. And yet, we might ask, what is the joy that does not come and go?

Part Two is about how sadness is a muse, teacher, gift, guide, and guru. It leads to some of the insights which, for me, have transformed my life, and to some of my favorite works of art and music, which seem to refract and communicate the poetry of loss. I'll also share a little of what I've learned from experiences of various shadow emotions, when I've worked with them in this way – and when I've failed to do so. Like the children's story of Eggbert the Cracked Egg, or the Japanese art of *kintsugi*, or the Rumi maxim that cracks make way for light, Part Two is about the gleaning of beauty from tears.

Part Three takes a more overtly mystical aspect. Coming to see the transparency of emotional states (negative and positive) yields, in this perspective, not only insight but a glimpse of the profound. Here, I focus more on Jewish traditions than on Buddhist or humanistic ones, with readings of sacred text, Hasidic teachings, and Jewish counter-traditions on the ways sadness can be a gateway to realization. The gates of prayer may be closed to many postmoderns; but the gates of tears remain open.

The redemption of ordinary sadness has not made me happy-go-lucky, or a soft-eyed yogi such as one sees on the cover of some New Age magazines. Happily or not, I am still sarcastic, hedonistic, ambitious, and frustrated in traffic. But over the years, I have experienced a kind of mental 'settling back' that is always accessible, and invariably reveals a certain flavor of poetry. In subtle, perhaps barely perceptible ways, I find this relinquishment has made me deeply joyful, content, and loving—not despite pain or loneliness, but because of them, *with* them, intermingling their flavors with those of my soul. My conviction is that one may have the direct, intimate experience of painful emotions—even grief, loss, and lack—as they are, as flavors or contours or tones of simply what is. And from that simplicity of coexistent presence there arises an underlying peace that lovingly accommodates the tears that fall. Fortunes are spent every year by people looking for a way to feel happy. If they would stop looking, they would find it.

The Gate of Tears

In memory of my parents

part one:
o p e n i n g

The only thing that keeps us from happiness is searching for it.

—Lama Surya Das

The Gate of Tears

What Always Is

This path is about what always is, and what sometimes is.

At the beginning of the spiritual path, there is sometimes a thirst for experience: perhaps profound, transformative moments of transcendence, or more mundane movements of the mind toward relaxation, contentment, healing, and joy. These are all attainable. Secular or religious, there is a human capacity to experience the extraordinary, from the simplest peace in the body after yoga, or the sense of pleasure when a poem has been finished, to extraordinary states of mind cultivated through intensive meditation, or entheogens, medicines, "drugs." All of us have known times of great joy and great loss, at which the numinous quality of human experience becomes apparent.

At such peak experiences, something shifts. Perhaps something is glimpsed about the nature of reality, or perhaps it's just a change in neurochemistry. Either way, human beings are marked by experience, changed by it.

Special experiences, however, are only around sometimes. There are also mouths to feed and promises to keep; injustices to mend and suffering to ease. There are families, responsibilities, mortgages, plans, forms, obligations, delights. Thus Jack Kornfield's memorable phrase, "after the ecstasy, the laundry."

What, then, is left of the drenched harmony of the summer's sunlight, when the winter slush has soaked my feet? Where is my spiritual enlightenment when my mother has died and I don't know what to do? When I feel alone? When I am weighed down by anxiety, or illness, or a sense of inadequacy and failure?

What *always* is?

I have been blessed with experiences that I would not have believed possible until I had them myself. Yet the greatest gift is in the laundry, not the ecstasy. By which I mean, in the midst of self-doubt, grief, sadness, shame, and loss. In the midst of these, alongside them, together with them, I also, sometimes, feel a sense of joy, acceptance, presence.

Thus the awareness that was once present only in the light of peak experience extends into places of grey and black. At first, the "holy" meant connected times, beautiful times, blissful times. Now it means anytime. Now the sacred changes its character, bursts out from its confines, embraces all of the notes of the symphony, including minor chords.

I have grown a little impatient with the ecstasies of the mystics. What about envy? What about anger? What about the times when we have suffered a loss and feel we cannot recover? For that matter, what about ordinary times, when, no matter how many poems I read about God or love or enlightenment, I still feel sad?

The kernel of the Buddha's four noble truths is that it is possible to accept pain, coexist with it, create a mental spaciousness large enough to contain it, and surrender the effort to be rid of it. Not to justify, explain, explore, reconcile, wallow, or dissipate it, but the opposite: to abandon any effort to be rid of this tone of my experience. It is what is. It is even beautiful. Sometimes.

Similarly, in contemplative Judaism, Jacob's amazed utterance that "God was in this place—and I, I did not know," has become a watchword for perceiving the sacred in all aspects of life, even those that are challenging, crushing. In this frame of reference, "what is" is the Divine, and It always Is. And in the yielding comes redemption.

When the desire to banish sadness is released, sadness cohabitates with joy, and gives birth to holiness. More moments merit being named as Divine. After surrendering the fight to stay afloat, I drown, but find I can breathe underwater.

To try to explain suffering is to attempt escape. But when explanation is no longer sought, the deep joy of the contemplative arises. Here we are; this is what is happening. It is not wrong or right, but whole and broken and sacred.

Happiness sometimes is; sadness sometimes is. But the kind of joy we are speaking of here always is, or at least is always available. It emerges when I say yes instead of no. And it resides in the spaciousness of space itself, through the gate of tears.

Right Now, It's Like That

Often, when sadness, loss, loneliness, or other modes of heartbreak arise, there's a tendency to try and find reasons—to *why*. Suppose one were to look in a different direction—to *what*. That is, what is the present-moment experience of these "unwanted houseguests," these difficult emotions that come, go, and sometimes come but do not go?

What might it be like to inhabit the experience itself, rather than the story accompanying it? Perhaps a constriction in the throat, or a heaviness in the chest. Possibly, in the mind, a certain flavor of consciousness, not unlike a flavor of food with more spice or salt than one might like.

It is unusual to do this. It is human nature to account for sadness by explaining it: I am sad because I have not succeeded in my career, I am lonesome because I am alone, I am crying because my mother has died. Such accounts can be helpful, but it is also helpful to stay, simply, with the present experience. What is going on? How many things can you tell me about what is actually happening right now?

And then, can you coexist with it? Of course, if you like, you can moderate the somatic expressions; if you find your jaw is clenched, unclench it. But what I mean is, is it possible to relate to these sensations, in body and mind, just as sensations of such-and-such a type, of this or that tenor or tone? Rather than something to be pushed away, might it be possible to simply let it be? To inhabit the truism of "it is what it is" and nothing more?

This is what I mean by what as opposed to why. The "what" is an ache, a pressure, a color of mind, a disposition of the heart. The "why" is a long, tantalizing narrative of how I got here, and how bad that is. The "why" may or may not be accurate, but it is much harder to live with than the "what."

You might even notice that the mental resting of being-with, of relaxing out of the effort to deny, is itself quietly sweet. Just in the relinquishment of pushing away, even without more, is a kind of joy. It is an unwording of experience, a pause in mental excavation.

Ajahn Sumedho, a monk in a Thai Buddhist tradition, likes to say, "right now, it's like that."

It is possible to cultivate this deceptively simple orientation of mind.

Simplify

The human mind has evolved into a very complex thinking, feeling, acting machine. When I say "I am sad," I am usually including a great deal more than the present experience of sadness: I am usually including the reason, the justification, how I feel about feeling sad. There's a lot going on.

If you like, see how many ingredients comprise your experience of sadness. What my parents did, what my ex did, what my boss did, what I did. What I want, what I won't get, what I wish I was feeling right now, who I wish I could be. Since I'm not your therapist and this isn't therapy, let's not go into the details. Just play 'catch and release' with your mind. Catch the thought, notice it, release it.

The way through the gate of tears is to drop the explanations and justifications, the wishes that things were different than how they are. It is instead to accept the sadness as a present-moment experience. It is what it is. (I will use that cliché again and again.) Feel it in your body, at this present moment, and stay with it.

I predict that two things will happen.

First, the sensation will pass, and you will know that it is true what George Harrison and Gautama Buddha and Ecclesiastes all said: that all things must pass. "This, too, shall pass"—*gam zeh ya'avor*—is also an adage that Jews learned, most likely, from the Sufis: *in niz bogzarad*. Nothing endures. This is one of the primary insights of the Pali Canon of Buddhism, meant for good times and bad. You may find it helpful.

Second, you may come to experience sadness as just another flavor of reality, another tone of reality (I struggle for the right metaphor), neither to be embraced nor to be avoided. Nor to be embellished, wallowed-in, avoided, shamed, pushed away. One can make peace with it. It will not necessarily get better. But through this process of refinement, it will likely get simpler.

What is Spirituality?

What is spirituality? The word has as many meanings as it does practitioners. For some, it is something to do with having a certain kind of experience: relaxation, a sense of the profound, love, calm, balance, maybe even holiness. Many things can bring this about: hymns in church, yoga poses, painting, gardening, meeting friends, EDM concerts, sex, drugs, meditation, cigars. It's not the what, it's the how—and it's a short-term transformation. Before I did X, I was feeling A. After I did X, I felt B.

I am a fan of this kind of spirituality. It is healing, and if it makes you more compassionate, calm, and wise, keep it up.

But the spirituality of special experiences only goes so far. At a certain point, it becomes a dead end, with the practitioner always searching for the next high, privileging some experiences over others, and not really having a way to integrate peak experiences with the rest of life. Eventually, most people who stay on the spiritual path get over this form of spirituality.

Meditation, in the forms I've taught for several years, is generally less about having a certain kind of experience than relating to *any* experience in a clear, compassionate, non-judgmental way. It's not what's going on, it's how one is relating to it. Like many spiritual notions, this is quite banal when written out in a book like this. But it is transformative, and challenging, when put into practice. Through one or another method, the mind's incessant stream of though is gradually slowed down. Over a period of time, a deep calming of the mind takes place, and an ability arises to see things more clearly. That calm and clarity are themselves quite pleasant, but their main benefit is what they reveal: the way things change, patterns of mind, beauty and dysfunction in the world, and the way the 'self' is more porous than it sometimes seems. This "seeing" deepens into an intuitive knowing, and the mind changes—evolves, if you like. It instinctively, intuitively learns to accept rather than reject or prefer. The change is quite remarkable.

As I said in the introduction, when I went on my first seven-day silent meditation retreat, I hoped, based on my decade or so of study of mysticism, that I would have some kind of mystical experience. I'd read accounts by mystics around the world reporting strikingly similar (though not identical) experiences: a sense of union with ultimate reality, an ineffable yet ineluctable sense of knowing, and so on. And while I didn't assume that these experiences would happen to me, I certainly hoped they would.

Well, they did—but for me, the ecstasy had to follow the laundry as well as precede it. First I spent several days seeing my own self-doubt, self-loathing, and other aspects of my "shadow" that my very busy mind ordinarily occludes. Those were days of tears, of hard work, and of a clarity of insight that I'd never before experienced. The same clarity of mind that made a single string bean taste like ambrosia also cast light on the shadows I'd been avoiding for years. To see both the light and the shadow, the necessary condition was to stop seeking, stop pushing away, stop arguing with my experience.

To understand deeply and intuitively, that even in moments of our greatest separateness, aloneness, or pain, there is nothing but God taking place—this is what lies through the gate of tears.

In this way, sadness is not an obstacle on the path; it is the path itself. "Faith sees best in the dark," remarked Kierkegaard in one of his sermons. Ordinary sadness, everyday melancholy, the quiet, small pains of life, as well as the more profound losses that are part of human life, are the places in which the real spiritual work takes place. Not the coloring of life by seeing it through rose-colored glasses, but the clear, transparent presence of being with life as it actually is.

Easy words to say. Difficult to apply.

Feeding the Birds

My partner Paul loves feeding the birds in our backyard. We bought a birdfeeder a few years ago, and now I know a lot about chickadees, nuthatches, and titmouses. It makes me love him so, to watch him this delighted and happy. God, am I lucky.

I have to admit, there is something captivating about watching these tiny birds alight on the feeder, grab a sunflower seed, fly off, and crack the seed against a tree branch. Once in a while, there's some drama (a woodpecker, a bluejay) but it's actually the mundane life of this mini-ecosystem that's so entrancing.

I suspect it's evolutionary: For millions of years, it's been to our species' advantage to observe little critters. It's pacifying, and absorbing, because we've been bred to find it so.

Yet there is also something profoundly comforting about watching the birds go about their lives. Though they are not silent, they are devoid of language. They have their habits, attachments, and social codes, but all of them are distant from us, and little understood—by most of us anyway. With them, life goes on.

Everyone knows this, of course, but knowing and seeing are different things. There is conceptual knowing, and there is direct, experiential knowing. It's a simple thing, watching birds go about their business, but it's also profound; it enacts the truth.

A popular podcast recently said, "Death is only the end if you assume the story is about you." This assumption, too, is evolutionary in nature. Animals that don't fear death, die. So it's entirely natural to assume, intuitively if not rationally, that this story is about me.

The birds, however, do not care about me at all. In their obliviousness, there is a powerful comfort. That's right, the story is not about me.

Of course. the story not being about me is half of the matter—what I can do is the other half. And what I can do is make the birds happy. I can relate to the people you see on park benches, pockets overflowing with crumbs. The birds remind them that they are not invisible, not powerless. As Whitman wrote, the powerful play goes on, and you will contribute a verse. You do contribute a verse, you can productively disturb the universe, even if only to some birds.

Feeding the birds does not address the causes of suffering, or process it, or make it go away. Sometimes, it's a reprieve. Sometimes, it simply exists alongside the pain, in a kind of harmony with it.

The Cliché of the Present Moment

Eckhart Tolle—yes, Oprah's guru—is known to have given the following instruction to his students: Turn your full attention to the Now, and tell me what your problem is.

Suppose I am feeling anxiety, worried about my friend who is ill. Tolle's instruction would be: Turn your attention to it—and keep it there. Don't wander off into elaboration, story, or anything else that pulls the attention out of your actual, immediate experience. Not the content of the worries for my friend, or plans, or possible outcomes. Just stay here, in what Tolle calls the "Now."

In the "present moment," there are the physical sensations of anxiety, a sense that they are unpleasant, a desire for them to go away, and, of course, a long story about the imagined future that can greatly magnify the anxiety if I decide to play it out.

Over time and with practice, it becomes gradually easier to 'catch and release' unhelpful thoughts as they develop. Just a few steps down the road, maybe just the introduction to the story—and you let it go. Sometimes I even catch myself at the story's headline: Oh, self-shaming. Oh, fear of the unknown. Oh, planning to try to somehow make things turn out okay. The Buddhist analogy for this is how a child learns not to touch the hot pan on the stovetop. At first, and maybe a few times, it is something which must be learned. Eventually, it becomes part of intuition.

Also over time, even the desire for the unpleasant feeling to go away—generally diminishes as well. You can learn to accept it, live with it, sink into it, or just let it be. It's here, in the "present moment," and that's just how it is. No point fighting with reality; reality will win. Gradually, this, too, becomes part of intuition.

In my experience, the physical sensations, and the unpleasant "feeling tone" that they carry, generally do not go away. That is what Sylvia Boorstein means, maybe, when she says that "In life, pain is mandatory but suffering is optional." The pain is what it is, but the experience of it, the relationship to it, can shift. They need not be quite as awful. In fact, the experience can also include a deep, abiding joy.

Now, I know that the phrase "the present moment" is a cliché, and an irritating one at that. As someone in love with words, I don't really like these three—and they're not even found in the Buddhist canon. They're pop-dharma.

Moreover, in my experience, you have to have had some kind of spiritual experience to even know what we're talking about. It doesn't have to be Buddhist or religious; it could be being "in the zone" on the basketball court or fully focused on a child. But if you've never felt this sense of ease, or flow, pablum about the present moment isn't going to help. It takes some experience to know what those words even mean.

But let's get over it. The "present moment" is a cliché, but the actual present moment is not. It is in fact possible to pause the mind's efforts to change what's going on, and in that pausing—that *Shabbat*—is bliss, nothing less. That never gets old, never gets clichéd.

And when the mind and heart are focused in this way, the sadness is what it is, and that's all. It's a collection of bodily sensations, a feeling-tone in the mind, and a story which we're not going into. It's like the wall being painted tan instead of white; the weather being cold instead of warm. With the preference for it to be other than it is temporarily sidelined, it's just like that, and that's all—and there is the joy of setting down the burden.

That is why the 'problem' disappears in the Now, when the present moment is an experience, rather than a cliché.

Sadness, like silence, may imply a lack. Sadness is the lack of joy, silence that of sound.

But when sadness and silence are seen simply, their negative space has a kind of elegance to it. The silence that contains sound—the vastness that contains space itself.

Your present-moment experience does not have to lack anything at all. Of course, we all want things we don't have, and don't want things we do have. That is human, and animal, nature. But we also have a capacity to quiet these desires, not by repressing them, but by letting them be—letting an internal silence grow—even if outside is noise.

Sadness has a spaciousness to it, like a great loneliness, soft and indigo. Just so.

Don't Believe Your Teachers

In the 1990s, a prominent teacher of what's called "New Thought"—a/k/a The Secret, the Law of Attraction, the Teachings of Abraham—told a group of gay men that they could cure themselves of AIDS by believing themselves to be cured. The catch was, they had to really believe it—and so many of them stopped taking medication (since why take medication if you're cured) and stopped going to doctors. These men died. Some were friends of my partner. And as far as I know, the teacher was never sued.

I bring this up to share advice that has been learned the hard way: Don't believe any teacher that promises you that you can get what you want.

In fact, while you're at it, don't believe any teacher at all. It's easy to mistake the cozy feeling of having a mother- or father-figure with having answers to questions that have none. It's also easy to mistake the feeling of having some control over your existence (as the Law of Attraction promises) for actually having it.

There are many words for such teachings, but I prefer the word "bullshit."

Of course, you can make yourself happier by focusing on positive things. A positive attitude does help healing (though a negative one can help be realistic about causes and consequences). Even smiling has been shown, physiologically, to bring about more happiness. You can fake it till you make it. And if New Thought helps you take ownership of your life, don't listen to me. I'm a teacher too, of course.

But the notion that You Can Get What You Want, in the larger sense, is outrageous. It's obviously and demonstrably false, and offensive, when applied to actual suffering. Did the people in the World Trade Center attract the planes? Did my mother attract cancer?

In fact, from a review of the evidence, it appears that Mick Jagger and the Buddha were right: You Can't Always Get What You Want. Sometimes you can, and if you try sometimes… well, you know the rest. But other times, the trying is only resistance to what is actually in front of you, and the resistance makes it worse.

Let's try the anti-law of attraction. Think of something you truly want. Now inhabit the sense of not getting it. Really visualize yourself not meeting your most profound desires. Skip the silly stuff—cars and whatnot—and go for the real. Love, success, health, long life, peace. If you feel sad about failing at your most cherished endeavors, allow the sadness to come without resistance. Make yourself at home there. It can be quite delightful, really. Listen to the sounds—of the room, of the city, of the birds chirping, whatever. All this will continue, and change, without you and your longing. Set down the burden.

Broken Open

When life is full of ease, spirituality is like cotton candy—fluffy, airy, and unserious. It's easy to mock the privileged, entitled yuppies in their yoga clothes, or the walking wounded going to endless, fruitless seminars. Not to mention the flocks in church. Good for them... I guess.

And then something happens. Someone gets sick, or a relationship ends. Or a pet dies, or I lose my job. Or a friend dies unexpectedly.

And then we go searching for meaning. Not answers necessarily—most educated people don't think that there are answers out there, let alone a puppeteer God beneficently ordering all of creations—but significance, meaning. Now the self-satisfied smirk of the critic melts into something less sure of itself. What can be understood in the midst of this tragedy, about the fragility of the human condition or the impossibility of holding onto it? And what are the forms which, over the years, people like me have created to contain this grief?

Thus pain becomes a gate to the recovery of the spiritual tones of living. I fail; I lose; and so I grow closer to the parts of myself which feel more authentic, more connected. Spiritual paths may not be as sophisticated or arch as other ways of being. They may be mocked in the pages of the *Times*. But at some point, most of us find ourselves broken—and hopefully broken open.

It's easy to be cynical about this sudden return to religious, spiritual, philosophical, or artistic homes long abandoned. We seem to be spiritual equivalents of fair-weather fans, clinging to a tradition or practice in our moment of need, then discarding it once again, when the moment of crisis has passed. Really, though, we are just flawed humans. To admit our inconsistency is only another necessary surrender. Fine, we are inconsistent. What do we sense to be true when we are at our weakest, our most open?

I got on the spiritual path because I was greedy: My mind thirsted for truth, my heart for love, my soul for experience, and my body for delight. Below the surface, there was a lot of suffering, but on the surface—if I'm honest—was a kind of hedonism. I was a FOMO mystic, Fearful Of Missing Out on any of what life had to offer.

Somewhere along the line I found myself among people seeking very different things. Some were working to address suffering—their own and others. Some were sincerely committed to something they understood as Spirit. But some were in search of pleasant delusions, or soothing reassurances that there was a purpose for everything, or promises that they could create their own realities, or some imagi-nary compensation for all they felt themselves to lack. How, I wondered, had I drifted into this?

The economics of spirituality was part of it: Answers sell better than questions, self-help better than poetry. Religion was too: moralism, promises of Sugarcandy Mountain, and myths that reify a per-sonal experience of joy into a God speaking to your soul. These all comfort, inspire, and guide many people, and so I hesitate to condemn them. God bless them, I guess.

But it was never my path, personally. I was never interested in My Flavor Above All Flavors, not because I was so moral but because it never made sense so. I also never believed anyone who said they'd really made it once and for all. I gave up looking for a guru long ago—it seemed an unrealistic expectation that my surrender to one person would somehow encompass and not flatten the Buddhist, Jewish, Earthy, queer, intellectual, hedonistic currents that keep me afloat.

Eventually, I grew out of my FOMO phase, though I still love a good mystical experience now and then. I'm not sure that's because I grew wiser; it's just that now I know I'm not missing out.

Ideas of what it is to be a "certain kind of person" are their own kind of orthodoxy, especially when it comes to the spiritual path. It's not just the religious fundamentalists who do this. Cynics and secularists do it, sure that spirituality is just for the weak-minded, and desperately working to find something wrong with it: narcissism, capitalism, dilettantism, Orientalism, whatever.

Spiritual people do it, too. As if it's only spiritual if it's in soft, soothing tones, or has a positive outlook, or subscribes to a total relativism in which every superstition is valid. As if there is no space within the great embrace of the contemplative life for football.

I love Ikkyu, the 14th century master of Japanese poetry, who scandalized his contemporaries (and, likely, ours as well, if they would know him) by cavorting with prostitutes, getting drunk, and railing against the institutional hierarchy of Zen Buddhism —all as a fully enlightened Zen teacher. "Don't hesitate to get laid—that's wisdom," he wrote in one short poem (translated here by Stephen Berg). "Sitting around chanting? What crap."

It's not that Ikkyu rejected Zen —quite the contrary, he lived his entire life as a Zen monk. He enlarged it; his Zen has space for anti-Zen, room for the empty hedonic, a surrender to the true omnipresence of the Question. Maybe the task of the spiritual seeker is to stop seeking; to give up any notion of knowing the right answer, or even of the right course of action. Justice and compassion remain, of course; but the pretense of piety is only an obstruction to the openness and acceptance that are the hallmarks of liberation.

Bumper Sticker: Religion is for people afraid of going to hell, Spirituality is for people who have been there.

The Wires are the View

I have told this story before. But I think it belongs here, told in a different way.

It had been a cool, early December day in Barre, Massachusetts, about ten years ago. I had spent the daylight hours, what was left of them, sitting in hour-long meditation sessions, and walking outside in the white, grey, and tan colors of Massachusetts winter. It had been a peaceful day, as I recall, about two thirds of the way through a 40-day meditation retreat at the Insight Meditation Society.

Forty days in silence. External silence, anyway, the better to hear the incessant noise of thought. The retreat had been profound, difficult, inspiring—par for the course. Four weeks in, I thought I had basically learned what I was going to learn. And then everything fell apart.

It began innocently enough: During a talk one evening, a teacher said that all of our habits, preferences, and opinions are conditions in and of the mind, and all of them can be changed. Dharma 101.

But I recoiled. Having spent over ten years trying to change my sexuality, having despaired of it to the point of suicide, and having finally given up trying to change and come out the other side healthy, sane, and whole, I felt as though I knew from experience both that some things cannot be changed and that to say it can be is enormously harmful. Even if sexuality is a phenomenon of the mind and not the body, sexual orientation is effectively hardwired in—for me, anyway, and for many other queer people. Trying to change it is as healthy as trying not to breathe.

So I was triggered. And so when the Dharma talk was done, I spent the next half-hour in walking meditation, furious at the ignorance of this teacher. I paced back and forth, noting a whole lot of anger, and getting lost in it more often than not. But then, literally mid-step, I realized how attached I was to the belief that sexuality cannot be changed. It wasn't just some intellectual difference I had with the teacher—I was really attached to my view. I had something at stake.

Then, in the next thought, I realized that I was so attached to my story that sexuality is unchangeable because I would change my sexuality if I could.

Which was shocking. At the time, I was the director of a national queer organization, and I've long been someone whose work and life is deeply gay-positive and celebrates the erotic and spiritual possibilities of being queer. I celebrate my sexuality, and recognize it as a unique gift. But here I was, realizing that a part of me was still self-hating, still telling myself that I'd rather be different. Here is what I wrote in my journal that night:

I'm tired of hating myself.

I'm tired of wanting myself to be straight, even a little.

I'm tired of "all things being equal, I'd prefer."

That night was a dark one. It's not that I even believed the self-hatred—I just could not believe that it was present at all. How could this be?

As I lay restless that night, I watched—and was often caught in—a caravan of thoughts and judgments: how I felt rejection, how I felt I'd disappointed my parents, how I'd failed. And I saw that "being gay" just felt bad, in a stupid, non-rational way, because people have told me so for decades. Intellectually, of course, I know not to believe them, but on a gut level, I felt unloved, unsuccessful, unappreciated. More from the journal:

> *Look at how much bullshit I still believe… I hate the hatred. It*
> *makes me feel unlovable. It makes me feel like a fraud. It makes*
> *me feel like I can never be enlightened, and have no business*
> *being a spiritual teacher.*

This, though, was progress. At least there was a recognition of the feelings. At least I wasn't believing them. Even then, I could tell that I was already not as swallowed by the feelings, or aversive to them, as I had been in the previous entry.

So, I tried working with this cluster of negative emotions—self-hatred, self-loathing—in the way I have described in this book. I wanted to see, even if only out of curiosity, if I could make space even for the self-hatred. I asked myself: Can I be with it? Can I accept it—not in the sense of saying the demon's okay—but just acknowledging its presence, and letting it in without pushing it away? Could I just name it—self-hatred—without wanting to push it away?

As I sat with these feelings, felt them in the body, accepted them, "loved them to death," something remarkable happened. I saw right through them. I saw that this sense that the self-hatred was "deep down" was bullshit. The geology of the self is a fiction. Deep down inside what? All that was actually going on were various beliefs and feelings. One belief (gay is bad) had the character of being long-held, another (gay is good) didn't. But the former belief wasn't really deeper or truer; on the contrary, I knew it to be the product of societal fear and delusion. It just happened to be older. There was no "deep down" —only the sense of it from time to time.

Here's a desire, here's a fear, there's a thought. Some thoughts feel deep, some shallow—but those are just sensations, nothing more. The feeling-tones are not reliable judges of value. For me, this was a radical rejection of a view of the self that seemed, to me at least, to be everywhere. "Trust your heart," people say. As if, the feeling accompanied by a certain feeling-tone ("deep down") is somehow more reliable than a feeling without it. You can be certain and be wrong, as John Kerry once said. Something can seem like a Divine voice, but really it's just how you were taught when you were three.

From the perspective of the Gate of Tears, a feeling-tone is a feeling-tone, and that's all. Just like anything else, the invitation is to be with it, not to listen to it, not to ignore it, not to push it away, not to repress it, not to act on it.

I lay in bed. The world seemed to be slipping away into a kind of moral anarchy. (As I've described in another book, that sensation may, itself, have been part of the unfolding of the contemplative path.) If I can't "trust my gut," what can I trust?

Actually, I knew what to trust. With calm and equanimity, it was easy to see which views led to more love and more compassion, and which led to more greed, hatred, and delusion. I didn't have to rely on the mystical movements of the soul; just reason and discernment. Of course I wouldn't always get it right, but the process was clear. Quiet, contemplation, reflection, being-with, allowing. Even now, there is a peace that awakens when I consider it.

That evening, I sat outside to watch the sun set. IMS faces west across a large valley, so often the sunsets were beautiful, and although it wasn't quite Buddhist equanimity to lust after beautiful sunsets, I did it anyway. Unfortunately, where I was sitting, a line of telephone wires was blocking the view, so I thought I might move to a different spot. But then, the wires blocked the view there too.

And then I got it. The wires weren't blocking the view, the wires were part of the view. I might prefer a different view, of course, one that conforms to images from postcards or fairytales, but this is the one that is. And likewise, the guilt, the self-hatred: These, not just the states of ecstasy and joy, are sometimes the view. The practice is to build a steadiness of heart to invite them in, rather than deny them or push them away. Just as when you're looking at a sunset, you don't have to resent or avoid or ignore the wires 'in the way,' but can instead accept them, and not worry about them so much. The wires are part of the view.

Then I went back to meditating.

Home

Walking through the gate, each step is the destination. No longer seeking for the promised land of others, now the soul seeks only the promise in the land she inhabits.

It is as if heaven becomes auditory: the pregnancy of a silence that can coexist with every timbre. No melody or lyrics can reflect the peculiar non-solitude of living with the sense of the sacred; there will always be an unintended counterpoint, a dissonance caused not by the natural fluctuations of rhythm and tone, but by the forcible insertion of intentionality and purpose. It will never work. Occasionally, of course, there will be serendipitous harmonies between 'ought' and 'is.' But just as often, there will be abrasions, scrapes, and even bruises—non-melodic noise that is rationalized away with one of the many rhetorics of incipient fundamentalism.

But through the gate, when she has stopped insisting that music is meant to sound a certain way, then, by precisely through silence, the spirit takes on every shape of composition. Atonality dances with Mozart; the djembe falls in with the flute. There is a delight in the sweetness of these sounds, as it is written: The messiah is the one who unites the world in song.

Through the gate is the gate itself, because there is nowhere that one feels required to go. Outwardly, the pilgrimage seems to continue: more steps, more tasks, more of the day-to-day. But inwardly, in the only spaces where the journey has ever made sense at all, the character of travel has shifted. Usually imperceptible to the outside world, a different quality of being has taken hold: one which no longer needs to go anywhere because it, she, is home.

Insight

The allowing of heartbreak is also its unveiling. Sometimes pain can be indistinguishable from the one experiencing it: It swallows me, I sink into it, I become it.

But the sense of union is delusory. What is actually arising is not coextensive with the mind (let alone with "me"). It is a condition, or set of conditions, that comes and goes. It can be seen; given space; the gateway can open wider.

"This is sadness" rather than "I am sad."

In my experience, this is not a simply semantic distinction. In the latter case, there is the postulating of the "I," and the immersion of it in the dye of sadness. This "I" is thoroughly tinted by the pain it is experiencing. It is, in the colloquial expression, overwhelmed.

But suppose the sadness, grief, anger, loss—suppose the pain is given space, as if perceptually, as if expanding the visual horizon to include the ground as well as the figure. Suppose there is enough spaciousness, in this imagined field of vision, for it to simply exist as it is: caused, appearing, unfolding, changing, eventually passing, perhaps reappearing. The imagery of "overwhelmed" implies a small "I" drowned in what has overwhelmed it. But that is just imagery (and having one nearly drowned in whitewater, I find it a little over-indulgent). A different image is of the storm raging against the background of a vast, empty sky. The storm is a phenomenon that occurs, changes, and passes. It is caused by conditions, and is itself the cause of other conditions. It is, in this sense, an object of attention rather than the state of the self. This is sadness. This is fear. This is loss.

Notably, sadness is not among the traditional hindrances to meditation, such as anger, restlessness, and doubt. It can be meditated-on, meditated-with. And then much of the Dharma becomes easily visible. This is suffering, the first noble truth; here is craving, the second noble truth.

And it is interspersed. There are infinitesimal breaks in the clouds: moments of perception, sensation, and thought. Quiet attention reveals them, and perhaps offers brief instants of relief. Here, too, more like a storm in the sky than a wave that overwhelms.

It is not necessary to have the sense of endurance, or suffering, or putting up with a difficult, unwanted, unfortunate emotion. It is possible, as the iconoclastic Dharma teacher Shinzen Young says, to "love it to death." This is true not only of specific emotions but of the whole, endless play of them, generally mistaken for a self. "It took me 15 painful years of misguided meditation," Shinzen said, "to finally realize that you can't hate your limited identity. You have to love your limited identity—love it to death."

The Banality of Awakening

I have trouble with titles. Fortunately, as a columnist, I don't get to write my own headlines, but when it comes to books, I tend to go back and forth a lot. Each of my books had half a dozen working titles, including this one. There's the catchy one, the irreverent one, the trying-to-be poetic one; the words never quite seem to cohere tightly enough. And then there's the subtitle. For this book, I considered the following:

Enlightenment in a Minor Key

Spiritual Paths and Everyday Sorrows

Letting Sadness Be

An Unusual Path to Liberation

The Radical Path to Awakening

Meeting Sorrow and Joy along the Spiritual Path

The Counterpoint of Redemption

On the Redemption of Ordinary Sadness

Spiritual Paths and Ordinary Sorrows

Do the languages of spiritual commerce matter? Sure, if you want books to be read. And nothing sells like mystery. The secret, the code, the power. But what good are those esoteric secrets really supposed to do, all the formulae or hidden correspondences? I've sometimes wondered how much of the path simply boils down to whether one is okay or not okay. Perhaps there are cosmological or theological verities as well, but to me, the psychological account seems sufficient. Are you, in this moment, okay (as you are, as it is) or not okay (sinful, lacking, fallen, not as it should be, not the way God wants)? *The Gate of Tears* is simply being okay with whatever is actually going on. (Or if you like, *Loving What Is*, in Byron Katie's words—though I think that may set the bar too high. I'm still working on Tara Brach's *Radical Acceptance*.) That okay-ness includes the sense that something is not okay—the sense of longing, or anger, or grief. Being okay includes being okay with not being okay. And thus, perhaps, not feeding it more.

Yet in my experience, there is a certain kind of secret, because the attitude of relation to experience is so subtle; it is the slightest inflection of perspective that transforms. As I've said elsewhere, true secret wisdom is experiential wisdom. That's why it can't be recorded. If you walk the path, you'll see.

As an artist of words, I love linguistic profundity. Unfortunately, many of the deepest truths have the ring of banality, until they are experienced.

Don't Worry, Be Unhappy

As long as I persist in thinking my sadness, anger, and dissatisfaction ought to stop, it is unlikely to stop. The engine turning the wheel is nothing other than the desire to escape from it. It's as if there is an impulse to push, and push, and push, always trying to move away from this unbearable grief.

On the spiritual path, there's a tendency to exchange gross futures for finer ones. The masses imagine some future time or place in which everything will be perfect, in which they will be happy, rich, loved, sexy. Ah, but the elite, we are profound, and above all that. We're going for spirituality. "If I only meditate more, then I won't feel so angry. I will be a more spiritual person."

From a remove, it is obvious that exchanging delusions is not really the point. Sadness, anger, and pain can only be redeemed when they are fully accepted. There is no 'redemption' in the sense of exchange, no emotional alchemy that is as permanent as we would like it to be.

Of course, therapy, a mental health regimen, a physical health regimen, joyful activities, being in nature, cultivating healthy relationships, sex, consent, justice—these practices can help us function better, live more fully, lighten the load of everyone else, and enjoy more of the delights in the world. Please: Get healthier! Work on your stuff! Make changes in your life!

But there will always be transient mind-states, and some of them will have flavors that we are conditioned to want to avoid. Get used to it. It doesn't mean you're doing anything wrong. Relax. Don't worry. Be Unhappy. It's what humans do, sometimes. Life is generally unfair. Illness and death exist. And there will be no explanation that really explains it away.

So—relax. It's hard feeling rejection, or loneliness, or loss. But we do not have to also feel bad about feeling bad. That extra layer—that *can* be unlearned.

And then, what's left? Yes, the cliché again—the present moment. It is always now. Or God. Or whatever. Fortunately, no deficit of irony can spoil it. This is about what always is, after all, so laugh all you want. You can banish your god-consciousness, your sense of the sublime, your respect for creation; you can deny, curse, doubt, reject. You can make it very hard on yourself. But it doesn't matter. the primary condition of freedom is always here.

So relax.

Yoga for Pessimists

Okay, try this.

Relax, allow your gaze to rest, not on one particular object, but just taking in wherever you are. Feel your body. Then say, slowly:

Things haven't turned out so bad, have they?

Comparison

Sadness is not comparable. Is it possible to quantify the pain of one who has lost a child, and to then compare it to my lesser pain of losing a parent? Or the lesser pain of losing a job?

Even if it were, does the existence of greater pain make lesser pain somehow unjustified? Am I not "entitled" to feel sadness, because someone else is sadder?

Comparing is a fool's game. Either the other people are more successful, or more loved, in which case, woe is me. Or maybe I'm ahead, in which case I can be grateful and patronizing, or selfish and superior—neither of which strikes me as really winning the game.

Ironically, the comparative enterprise is also a form of denial. I have it bad, but not as bad as X. As if the heart only breaks when it is justified. Eat your peas, someone is starving somewhere.

From the perspective of justice, it is important to remember that our pain is not as great as that of a political prisoner, or a victim of oppression, or someone struggling with subsistence and survival. Taking a reality check is a good antidote to the potentially absurd narcissism of privilege. It also might help dislodge self-pity and, more importantly, inspire action and engagement.

But in the pursuit of justice, pain and equanimity are both allies. Suffering, when experienced rather than repressed or denied, is an engine for the generation of compassion. And equanimity enables the capacity to act upon it. I couldn't have done the justice work I've done professionally for fifteen years without the counterweight of mindfulness and equanimity. There is not a shortage of anger, but a surfeit of it.

Those who criticize 'bleeding hearts' survive in the world by shutting off their hearts. Perhaps if they would open them for just a moment, their policies of cruelty would be too painful for them to bear.

That is the gate of tears: to experience the heart, not to minimize it, not to compare it to others' pain for any purpose—not for self-justification, not for self-pity, not for self-criticism, not to make the self feel better. All of these acts are attempts to make the ego feel better. Even the act of self-criticism ("Stop feeling so sorry for yourself!") is intended, perversely, to make the self feel better: by punishing the ego for inappropriate self-pity, the goal is to scold it into stopping the self-pity and starting to feel more appropriately happy. Smiling now?

This is not the gate to greater liberation. Yes, your suffering is not as bad as others, who deserved it even less than you do. And it is definitely worse than that of the lucky, fortunate few. Does that help? No. These comparisons are worse than pointless.

Outside of comparing mind, there is just what actually is happening, without decoration and elaboration, and a subtle resting of the mind that arises when the impulses to hold or flee are relaxed. This experience is what it is. It may be joyous, or sorrowful, or painful—but if there is no need to hold the joy or heal the pain, there is only perfection in imperfection. Sadness is to be embraced because it invites us to embrace the whole.

So I have found it more helpful to release the desire to compare, enlarge, or minimize. I strive to enter the sadness itself, experience it for what it is, with whatever tears or lack of tears coalesce. The sadness of the monk who has lost his son, and yours, and mine, is part of the unfolding of how the world is. Dharma. God. Simply the way things are.

You Are Entitled to Be Miserable

One teacher of mine observed how it's so important, sometimes, to justify our feelings. We say, defiantly, "I am entitled to be sad!" as if someone is trying to take our sadness away from us.

Well, don't worry. No one is. You can be as sad as you like. Happy now?

The Opposite of Wallowing

Wallowing in sadness is the opposite of entering the gate of tears.

Wallowing is dredging up the story: Woe is me, I've lost this job, this lover, this friend. Woe is me, I am severely ill. Woe is me, my sports team lost the sports game. Profound or ridiculous, the movement is the same. The act of wallowing is an act of moving away from the present-moment experience into a thousand justifications for it, attempts to wriggle out of it. Paradoxically, wallowing is a kind of avoidance.

Wallowing is also a kind of sustenance; it nourishes the pain. And like a perverse mother bird, it does whatever it needs to do in order to feed it. The stories of wallowing are, objectively speaking, highly unreliable. It's as if there's a "pain translator" in the mind that will find a story, any story, to articulate and increase the quantum of pain. My fault, her fault, anxiety over this, fear of that—the only truth here is the pain. And when one is in pain, one is the least qualified to evaluate and articulate it.

Perhaps, if self-compassion is not adequate to drop the activities of elaboration, simple skepticism is. 'This investigation is unlikely to be fruitful.'

Likewise scolding and judgment, which act like Tolkien's Ring of Power, corrupting the one who wields them. The Buddhist analogy is that anger is like a hot stone; you may or may not burn the person you want to hit with it, but you're sure to burn yourself.

Okay—this happened. It is not okay, and it is okay that it is not okay. Okay—I can coexist with it. It is what it is. I'm here. It's here. We're here.

Sylvia Boorstein, another of my teachers, is fond of saying, "It's not what I wanted, but it's what I got."

Get Over It

I used to think that if I got over my sadness, anger, or humiliation too quickly, then it was not okay to have felt it in the first place. "No, no—this is *serious*—it's not something that I can just snap out of or get over."

Snapping out of sadness does not render it unserious. It just means the feeling has passed. Don't worry about the dignity of your sadness, or the indignity of getting over it. Let your friends think you are fickle because yesterday you seemed so upset yet today you are laughing. See if you can shrink your recovery time to a matter of seconds. Don't make an idol out of a mind-state. It was here, and now it's gone. To the wish that we could keep feeling a different way, the way we felt when all was sad and holy and quiet—to *that* I would say: Get over it.

Change the Channel

The basic practice of opening the gate of tears—being with, coexisting with, letting be, making space for unwelcome emotions —is what meditators practice every time they sit down on the cushion. A thought comes up: Be with it, and it goes. A pain arises: Be with it, and it goes.

Or it doesn't. Sometimes, the only thing that's happening is the pain—maybe in the back, or the leg. All you're doing is sitting there with the pain, and you're no longer learning anything.

At a certain point, it becomes skillful to "change the channel," so to speak; you change the conditions; you reach for an antidote. Maybe you shift your posture, ever so slightly. Maybe you spend a moment thinking about how to prevent such pain in the future. This doesn't make you a bad meditator—it makes you a balanced one. Especially if you undertake the antidote without expectation of it necessarily working. You add the antidote and see what happens.

Likewise through the gate of tears. It's not that sadness is so great, or better than other states of mind. Take a break sometimes. Don't decorate self-pity with fancy rhetoric. Go out and get some exercise. See friends, or a movie. Eat, drink, enjoy.

Don't worry, your grief is still real, still dignified even if you break it up with laughter. When it is time to let grief go, even for a moment, please do let it go.

Sometimes, you might even notice that the sadness really was an emotional manifestation of a physical condition. Maybe you were just tired. Or hungry. Or lethargic. All the sound and fury was just a story. Perhaps the ghosts who troubled Scrooge on that Christmas Eve really were just a bit of undigested meat.

Other times, the sadness returns. It isn't just indigestion. But the impermanence of sadness can still be noticed and learned from: It was here, then it was gone, now it's here. It can all feel very impersonal, in a good way. It's just what happens. You tried an antidote, it worked for a while, and then it didn't. In the meantime, you can be present in the break time, enjoying yourself, sensing whatever joy, or relief, or dark humor, or love has parted what had seemed to be an uninterruptable continuum of misery. That is a very helpful thing to see.

Empty Boat

Ram Dass gives the following advice on human relationships:

Imagine you are in a boat, floating in a thick fog. Through the mist, you barely make out the form of another boat, and you realize it is advancing towards you on a collision course.

"Stop!" you shout. "I'm here!"

The boat continues. "Stop! Please! Hey!"

The boat continues to advance. You become angry, upset, anxious. "Dammit, don't you see there's someone here!" You can't believe the idiocy of the captain of the other boat; his obliviousness; her lack of regard for you. Yet just as the boat is about to collide, you realize it is empty.

Maybe give that story a moment to settle.

Human beings get hurt by other human beings. This is what happens sometimes. There is also a narrative, however, about how this transpires: This person is a jerk, is a Republican, is a Democrat, is a liar, is a self-involved narcissistic idiot. Fill in the blank.

What is really happening, though, is that countless causes and conditions have brought this person and you together—and none of them really *is* you or the other person. Take a look at this some time; you can be as judgmental as you like. My co-worker is acting this way because of her dysfunctional family system. I am acting this way because I am hungry. You don't have to be right (in fact, you probably won't be)—the point is to see, directly, that there's no one there guiding the other boat. There is just the boat, being pushed by currents. Empty phenomena, rolling on, says the Dharma.

Cause and effect, not self. It's all around us; cause and effect, cause and effect. Your pain, their pain, skillful actions, unskillful actions. Our intersections with one another are each a nexus of a billion causes and effects. This action happens, I feel hurt.

There is a story of a Zen master who learned that his son had died (some say it was a Tibetan monk; other say it was a student whose master had passed). He began to weep. His students asked him, "Roshi, why are you crying?" because they knew him to be enlightened and enlightened people are supposed to be beyond all that. He answered, "Because I am sad."

What Equanimity is Not

Equanimity is not the banishment of sadness. It is the acceptance of sadness for what it is, and the letting go of the desire for it to end.

Similarly, equanimity does not involve a lessening of emotion. Mass media representations often depict equanimous meditators as peaceful, Zenned-out, happy, privileged, rich, white, female, young, and attractive. No wonder a million people are taking it up every year.

But that imagery is inaccurate. How repellant it would be if it were true—if the contemplative life were about ignorance, suppression, and fakery. Yes, there is relief, respite, and peace. But in the West, at least, to feel intensely the *suchness* of the world, to "suck the marrow out of life," is part of what it means to be alive.

Enlightened people experience joy, sadness, ecstasy, and pain. Their equanimity consists in accepting all of these transitory mind-states for what they are, neither grabbing the positive ones nor repelling the negative ones. To me, this makes enlightenment seem more remarkable but also more possible.

Intimacy with the Enemy

Here in the West, most people become interested in Buddhist-derived meditation practices—mindfulness chiefly among them—to relieve a very specific type of suffering: stress. As it happens, mindfulness relieves stress in two very different ways. Moment to moment, the concentration of the mind—gathering the mind together, quieting down the noise—itself brings a kind of relaxation. But over time, a different shift takes place: a settling back of the mind from the constant push and pull of trying to manipulate experience.

In the first aspect, suffering ends temporarily, as the practitioner creates a kind of island of peace. But this wears off quickly.

In the second aspect, suffering continues for a long time, though the relationship to grief, loss, pain, physical ailments, loneliness, and sadness does gradually shift. Bad things continue to happen. An end to suffering really means an end to grabbing onto those mind-states, wishing they would go away, and experiencing suffering because they don't conform to our wishes.

The gate of tears is traversed by a path of surrender. Paradoxically, by leaving negative mind-states be, suffering can indeed lessen in intensity. There is still sadness, or loneliness, but it is experienced without the stories and identities that perpetuate it. When it is experienced in this way, it is simply what is unfolding, in whatever flavor it has. You can learn to become intimate with your internal emotional enemies.

Not just wisdom and peace arise as a result, but also compassion for oneself and others. Nothing really changes along the contemplative path, yet everything changes. Sadness remains, yet it is experienced as great openness, as just this.

Redeemed Sadness is Remembering

In the throes of sadness, it is very difficult to know the real causes of what one is feeling; the storm (or the fog) is too intense to see clearly. Yet it is at precisely such moments that the tendency arises to be one's own analyst, to tease out the reasons and the justifications, to mull it all over, to ruminate and wallow and analyze, as if the knowledge gained from doing so will somehow remove the burden.

In fact, the effort is part of the storm. It promises a kind of insight, but is instead a kind of forgetfulness. And what it has forgotten is the simplicity of being itself; the presence, or Presence, of all that is beyond the stories of my own perceived injustices. It has forgotten the "And": that all of this storm is raging, and that it is raging within a vast sky.

Deep sadness and deep joy are thus parallel occasions of remembering.

Just So

I sit quietly, listening to the falling leaves—
A lonely hut, a life of renunciation.
The past has faded, things are no longer remembered.
My sleeve is wet with tears.

The Zen poetry of Ryokan (1758-1831) evokes the ineffable *suchness* —the sense of just-so—that is characteristic of Zen consciousness of emptiness. The leaves fall, the trees fall, at once empty and full, meaningful and meaningless. "Illusion and enlightenment? Two sides of a coin.... All day I read the wordless sutra; all night not a thought of Zen practice," Ryokan writes in another poem.

Zen is often regarded as teaching paradox. Really, though, the sense is tathata (or dharmata), which means just-so-ness, or suchness. Emptiness and form, delusion and enlightenment—

there are, to be sure, plenty of explications of the seemingly paradoxical ontology of these dualities. But ultimately, the tathata of how this is so must be gestured toward, not explicated. Perhaps this lack of pedantry is why the aesthetic of Zen is so appealing, even in its ridiculous commercial reductions ("Find Your Zen"). The simplicity of it is in Ryokan's poem. The falling leaves are not symbolic. The loneliness is direct, unencumbered by florid elaborations. As the artist and author Frederick Franck put it, "Zen is the unsymbolization of the world."

The tears are just so. They are not tears—they are empty phenomena rolling on, devoid of separateness, entirely dependently originated—and they are tears.

Many of Ryokan's poems are about loneliness. Many celebrate the hermit's life, but more, I think, describe its loneliness. We do not find here a Thoreauvian enjoyment of the woods (but then, Walden Pond was only a few miles from his family's home), nor an erasure of the loneliness, nor, exactly, a complaint about it either. It simply *is*, and as a result, is simply.

> In the blue sky a winter goose cries.
> The mountains are bare; nothing but falling leaves.
> Twilight: returning along the lonely village path.
> Alone, carrying an empty bowl.

> Foolish and stubborn—what day can I rest?
> Lonely and poor, this life.
> Twilight: I return from the village
> Again carrying an empty bowl.

I suppose it is possible to read these verses—translator John Stevens labels them "Empty Bowl: Two Poems"—in a plaintive tone, but I don't think that's the intention. In the first stanza (or poem) conveys the *dharmata* of the outside world. The winter scene is beautiful, though also stark. Hermits subsist on donations; if Ryokan's bowl is empty, he is hungry. The mountains are bare and so is his stomach.

In the pop understanding of Zen, that stanza is sufficient. You can imagine the scene in a Japanese painting: the path, the near silence outside. But the second stanza is also part of the emptiness/fullness. The *anatta*, non-selfness, of loneliness is true within as well as without. Ryokan's sense of being foolish, stubborn, tired, lonely, and poor—these, too, are empty phenomena rolling on, both real and unreal.

Do you see the difference? Pop Zen is an exterior aesthetic, often presuming (or helping to create) a tranquil interior. Real Zen is interior as well as exterior emptiness. Feelings of loneliness and foolishness are not whitewashed like a minimalist "Zen" design aesthetic. They're not embellished, either. They simply *are*, inside and outside, the arising of regret and the cry of the winter goose.

Pop Zen and pop spirituality have the potential to deny or denigrate the flux of the interior life. Real Zen and what I understand as authentic spirituality coexist with the flux, each color empty/full, just so. The tranquility of the contemplative life is not that everything is calm and simple, like a "Zen" water faucet—but that the contours that are present are neither denied nor elaborated upon. That is its simplicity.

Ending the War

Sadness and other painful states of being are a gate because they offer the opportunity of coexisting with everything, of making peace, of ending the war with experience. The sadness is felt, as is the joy—but it has the characteristic of spaciousness, meaning, the feeling takes place without overpowering or drowning the person who feels it.

This is quite different from the spirituality of pleasant experiences, in which we prefer some states to others, and pursue the spiritual practices which bring them about. Like a lot of people, I prefer to feel ecstasy, connectedness, holiness, and serenity (sometimes all at the same time) and I know a variety of spiritual techniques to bring these states about, in myself and others. It's rather like pulling a lever: I have the ability to say and do the right things, and so I do them, and some percentage of the people I am with have certain lovely experiences.

I don't mean to belittle the authenticity or healing power of these experiences; I'm just noticing that they are conditioned by certain behaviors, and less special than some may think. Certainly less enduring. At a certain point, they lose their punch. And I have also noticed, as Rabbi Gershon Winkler likes to say, that "When you invite in the light, you invite in the shadow." I've found over the years that the higher my spiritual highs get, the lower the lows that follow. A nice weekend on the beach can leave you feeling a little sad the next week when you return to work. A mind-blowing ecstasy in which orgasmic joy fills your entire body can later leave you desolated. So, a word to the wise: Watch your heart.

Still, even a glimpse of light on a cold and dark day can be deeply and powerfully nourishing.

Certainly, I've not written this book because I have triumphed over sadness and never experience it; quite the contrary. Only by surrendering to the experience can the war truly end.

Letting sadness be is a form of not-knowing, not-seeking, not-desiring. Because sadness is almost reflexively judged by the mind to be unpleasant, allowing it is an act of mental withholding. All animals are conditioned to push away the unpleasant; it is a natural thing to do. So the mere non-act of coexistence requires a kind of negative effort. Such effort can sometimes feel like restraint, a forced tamping-down of the urge to eliminate the difficult. Yet even this restraint can be released, revealing only relaxation, only the peace of ceasing to struggle.

The cessation is sweet in itself. At last, the fight is over. Grief is here; I surrender. I give up, and in the giving up, I can rest.

But this surrender is not a defeat, because one's mental landscape is not a battlefield. Rather, what has surrendered is the egoic need to control, know, understand, and dominate. All of us have this need; as with pushing away that which is unwanted, the assertion of the self is present in everyone, male and female, "spiritual" and not. It is, however, only a need—only a mental pattern. The sense of surrender is that someone has done the surrendering. In reality, only a pattern has stopped.

And what remains when the dust-storm of ego has settled is a clearer vision, a more open vista. The storm wants to know, to understand; it wants to control and protect. As applied to sadness, it wants to know *why* there is sadness so it can stop it. It wants to eliminate sadness and replace it with anger, indignation, blame, or vengeance. So it undertakes the work of rationale in order to transform, because it knows what is best for us: not to host the unpleasant.

In contrast, the calmer, clearer mind allows itself to be overtaken, because it does not pretend to know what is best. It does not seek the destruction of that which is unpleasant, because wisdom has taught it that the effort of destruction is counterproductive, and obscures clear seeing. Of course, there is still some desire to feel better, but that desire is accommodated just as the sadness is: with equanimity and wisdom. I feel sad, I feel the desire not to feel sad, I do nothing but feel clearly and richly—and love.

The Experience of Liberation

The sadness is not the problem. The hatred of the sadness is the problem. The sadness is just a state of mind, heart, and body. It is a variation on a theme, a melody. In itself, it causes no suffering. Suffering derives from the momentum of dislike.

The experience of liberation is simply sitting back, setting down the burden, declining to push or pull. It is acceptance of that which is. No more is needed: no secrets or magic. And so, when sadness, like anything else, is fully accepted, enlightenment is present in that instant.

Perhaps, a moment later, the sense of peace departs. In which case, repeat the process of setting down the burden.

It is fine if this is merely the relaxation response, triggered by the release from tension. Who needs more? The tension of holding, of pushing away, and then... the release.

On the other hand, in my experience, it is the same every time, and yet blessed every time.

I should also be clear that I fail as much as I succeed. Often, the urge to explore why I feel sad, or what is wrong, or some other aspect of the story of sadness, is irresistible. Like anyone else, I indulge, cry, plan, and plot. What I have learned, however, is not to fight even the fighting—not to hate even the hatred. It happens, when the conditions are present, and my wishing it were not so only makes it worse. Other teachers, perhaps, can claim a better track record at the disciplines they teach. As for me, I stumble often—but even in the stumbling is the opportunity of non-resistance.

I also find—and I admit that I have not kept statistics—that after a period of sadness, inspiration flows. When the mindstate passes, and it does, the bliss of ordinary experience—reflections of light, smells of leaves—becomes almost palpable. I feel renewed, and creative. It's not as if fireworks go off and all is happy again. Rather, I have the experience of having settled in. The mood is what it is, and I have at last made my peace.

This is how sadness can become a gate: when it leads to realization. Yet the inaccuracy of the metaphor is this: One passes through a gate by positive action, by moving-through it into something else. Whereas the gate of sadness opens when one surrenders all action, and one does not move at all, but rather yields, and accepts where one is. This gate admits only those visitors who do not seek to enter.

The Gate of Tears

part two:
l i s t e n i n g

And in the silent,
scarcely moving times,
when something is drawing near,
I want to be among those who know secret things
or else alone.

Rilke, *The Book of Hours*, I.13

The Gate of Tears

A Winter Song

Do we suppose that only summer has its music? Is there not a poetry to winter, too, when days are short and the body wants fattening and rest—is this too not a kind of music?

I love the steam rising from laundry vents, the indoor smells of incense and firewood, the warmth of stew and meat, the embrace of a companion in bed on a cold, bright day. And I love, sometimes, the alterations in my mood: more solitude, more loneliness, more melancholy. They go together, the winter outside and the winter of the heart.

So not only acceptance, yielding, surrender—but also listening, learning, appreciation, and alchemy. A minor-key melody; a winter song; a solitary vision of salvation; a silent kind of beauty; something that births art, song, love.

As from a great altitude

"Over the last few days," Oliver Sacks wrote, after receiving a diagnosis of terminal cancer, "I have been able to see my life as from a great altitude, as a sort of landscape, and with a deepening sense of the connection of all its parts."

Sacks's eloquent essay in the *Times*, published about six months before he died, is, like much of his writing, gracefully articulate. Now he is the patient, the case study; he is able to see his life as if from above, rather than only from within. There is a wise objectification here: that is, a taking-as-object, an observing eye.

It is not that the gift of this perspective makes terminal cancer worth the exchange. Sacks is clear on that. There is no erasure of the pain, no false commerce between it and the insights it brings. There is only an acknowledgment that those insights do exist; that there is wisdom born of suffering.

There is wisdom, and calm, that flows from seeing one's life as if from a great altitude. One's roads are now appear plotted, the different territories of one's life in contiguity with one another. What was, at youth, an open horizon is now, from above, populated with loves, accomplishments, work, pain, joy, meaning.

Likewise the expanded relational space, so to speak, beyond the individual geography. There are things I did, and changed, and influenced, and things I did not do. Sacks writes in his essay that he is no longer following the political news—not because he doesn't care about the Middle East or global warming, but because these are now in the hands of others. Perhaps they always were. The seeing as if from above brings with it a warm sense of boundedness and relation. I did this, I influenced that, I touched this person—and also, there is so much beyond. I am not the sum total of significance. My impact is real, and limited.

In my own life, blessed with privilege and education and some abilities, I've often felt the disappointment of not doing enough, not being famous enough, not selling enough copies, not influencing enough people or events or movements. Some of this, I think, is authentically about the work, whether as an activist or a writer and rabbi. Most of it is likely about my ego, which has an infinite thirst for significance. No accomplishment is enough to be enough.

So it is a sweet corrective to try on Sacks's aerial perspective for a moment. The intuitive knowledge of limitation is a counterweight to the ego impelled to do it all, have it all. I experience it as not a contraction, but a relief.

The Companionship of Compassion

I'm riding the subway in New York, three weeks after my mother passed away.

My past experience of grief is that it comes and goes, arriving unexpectedly and often suddenly. Eventually, it comes less frequently. This process is similar, and today has been a mixed day. Not as hard as others, but a little subdued, a little grey. The winter weather is contributing, too; New York is full of slush, and of people bundled in black coats.

I'm on the subway home, having said kaddish (twice) at an Orthodox *minyan* downtown. It's ironic that my mother, a staunch feminist and egalitarian in all things Jewish, is now the impetus for me to spend so much time in Orthodox, mostly-male spaces. But it was still moving, in its way.

On the train, I start doing *metta* practice for the people in my car. *Metta*, in the Theravadan Buddhist tradition, is pretty straightforward; you focus on a person (or multiple people, in this case) and mentally express a wish of lovingkindness toward them. One (shortened) version, which I use now, is "May you be free from suffering."

It's not meant to be magic, not like superstitions about prayer having the power to heal. Rather, the point is to cultivate a sense of internal lovingkindness toward others. You repeat the phrases for awhile, try to mean it, and eventually you really do feel lovingkindness, compassion, and so on.

This time is like a *metta* home run. The car is full enough that I have to stand, so I look out over the people sitting, reading, playing games on their phones, and—although this is not the way the practice is meant to be done—imagine a little about what their suffering might be like. I wonder who else has suffered a loss recently. I don't make any eye contact (it is New York, after all) but glance at facial expressions. I picture people out of this subway car, enjoying time with family, or struggling to get by. Many people look very tired. I realize I am too.

May you be free from suffering.... May you be free from suffering. Over and over—not like a mantra, exactly, but repeated nonetheless, arhythmically, with the attention on the experience of lovingkindness.

I see a poster urging people to file their taxes and claim their refunds. "What will you do with your refund?" it asks. A family is pictured, and their reply is, "We're going to make rent this month." I reflect on that. It's not part of my experience; I'm not a one-percenter by any means, but I don't have to worry about making rent month to month. What is that like? The family has two kids. How much responsibility? How much anxiety? how much uncertainty? This is how most Americans live, after all;

I am privileged, fortunate, and in the minority. *May you be free from suffering,* I say to the parents in the poster. *And remember this politically,* I say to myself.

By the time the train has crossed from Manhattan into Brooklyn, I feel profoundly happy, and profoundly sad. Not alternating; together. I feel happy *because* I feel sad, and my sadness connects me to the people in the car, the people in the poster. Of course I have no idea how my experience compares with theirs. But by inhabiting my own pain, I find myself sincerely able to wish that the people around me be free from suffering. I feel myself healed, not by being mended, but by being open, raw, human.

Mustard Seeds

Another Dharma story on the solidarity of suffering, this time an ancient one.

In the Buddhist anthology known as the *Therigatha,* the 'Verses of the Elder Nuns,' there is mention of a nun named Kisa Gotami ("Skinny Gotami") who eventually attains perfect enlightenment. A commentary to that text contains her origin story that became a popular Theravadan Buddhist legend.

It runs as follows. Kisa Gotami was a poor woman with a single son who died in his childhood. Bereft, she carried his corpse around her village, begging for medicine. A wise man, thinking her deranged, told her to go see the Buddha, which she did. The

Buddha said he could cure Kisa Gotami's son if she would bring him a mustard seed from a house that has not known death.

She went in search of such a house. But of course, none could be found; everywhere she went, someone had lost, suffered, grieved. Understanding the universality of suffering and the nature of impermanence, she was able to bury her son, to see the Dharma, and to become a follower of the Buddha.

The consolation Kisa Gotami receives is not that her suffering does not exist; she does not make it go away. Rather, the consolation—the gift of her tears—lies in its universality. Yes, this is pain—and yes, all feel it.

I have been struck by the fact that Kisa Gotami lost a child specifically. As I have moved through the grieving process for my mother, I have drawn comfort from the sense that this is, in a way, how it ought to be. Parents get older and die. But for Kisa Gotami, it was not this way. Of course, in Axial Age India, children dying was far more common than today, but still, her story seems more remarkable for lacking the consolation of order.

So she becomes a nun, impelled by both wisdom and compassion: wisdom insofar as she understands impermanence on an intuitive level, compassion insofar as she sees how suffering is universal. Of course, none of this is said to make it worth it.

You probably know Leonard Cohen's version of the Rumi poem, that "there is a crack in everything," and that crack is how the light gets in.

The simplicity of this metaphor is amplified, I think, by Cohen's voice—already scratchy, almost whispered—when he recorded the song "Anthem," and thinner still today. Maybe even more expressive.

What Cohen also adds to Rumi is the sense of cyclicality. The birds sing at the break of day. "Start again," they say—though Cohen's delivery adds weariness to their hope. Don't dwell on what has gone, or what is coming. To start again is to start anew is to start now.

Injustice will come again as well; wars fought, the sacred objectified. In a sense, to "forget your perfect offering" is to mirror the world into which the offering is sacrificed. Both are cracked, broken.

In its way, theosophical Kabbalah presents a similar conception of the world: that everything is cracked, everything is broken, but amid the shards are sparks of the sacred. In Rumi (and Cohen), the cracks let in light from outside (or let light shine from within); in Lurianic Kabbalah, the cracked shells themselves contain residue of the holy sparks.

Psychologically, when the soul is cracked, it is cracked open— open to people beyond itself, intimations and subtle movements. This has been my experience; the spiritual truths and emotional bonds that appear in moments of my own breaking are indeed the ones that penetrate the shell.

E.B. White once remarked, "Genius is more often found in a cracked pot than a whole one." That may be true as well; perhaps not only poets, but geniuses too. For better or for worse.

At the same time, it is easy to fall in love with one's own woundedness, with the longing and the sorrow. That is not quite the path I want to walk. There is a sacredness to the wound and to the longing, but they are not wounds to be licked, over and over again. These shadow aspects are generative, but not when they are coddled and overly cherished. I prefer to imagine them as reservoirs, or perhaps springs; I am less interested in diving again to the source than in the abundance it brings forth.

Some interpretations of religion insist that the world is getting better and better, others (more popular today) that it is getting precipitously worse. Either way, the impulse toward millennialism seems universal; the insistence that there is a linearity to world history, as there is to our own lives, and that it will culminate in a kind of death—only to be followed be rebirth.

But the cyclicality of Cohen's anthem (like that of Ecclesiastes, which we will explore later) is a skeptical counterargument. What was, will be again—both in the repetition of tragedy and in the newness of the day. There is a comfort here.

Is the light a recompense for the crack? I wouldn't say. Is the heaven bestowed on Langston Hughes' lonely poetic voice better than love? Who has better luck?

For years, I wanted to obtain the measurement, to know whether I was doing better than the squares whose conventions I had either rejected, or been unable to fulfill. Fortunately, I have given up. The crack is, the light is; I cannot say whether it would be better not to have been cracked at all.

Priests demand perfect offerings, but I have none to give. Only cracked bells, some of which still can ring, off-timbre, as if in winter.

A Fan Letter

Music is a metaphor for the spiritual practice of sadness. There is no better analogy to the peculiar juxtaposition of spiritual sadness and joy than the heartsick beauty of music in a minor key.

Why certain melodies and harmonics affect us the way they do has been the subject of science and pseudoscience. One sad day, I suppose we will know the answer—but for now, the question retains its mystery. Yet, while we may not know why this is so, it is so. From the simplest melody of a flute to the polyphonies of symphonies and electronics, music is able to express certain inarticulable tones of the human heart. Perhaps it is no surprise that the inexplicable is most at home with the true.

Writing about music is like talking about wine; it is hard not to sound preposterous. Two minutes of Nick Drake's "Pink Moon" seem to say more about how sadness gives birth to beauty, how the aesthetic of melancholy alchemically transforms pain into salvation, than all the reviews in the world—all the better because it, like the best songs of sadness, has but the slightest lyrical connection with its actual subject matter. Nick Drake, incidentally, developed his own distinctive guitar tunings, so that he could play aspects of major and minor chords together.

Like the Blues, which speaks of all forms of human suffering in the analogical language of love, the best sad songs are oblique, deliberately aiming slightly wide of the mark. The nearest reckonings are often those with no words at all: only music, or the minute inflection of a master singer.

In the music of sadness, what is not said, then, carries as much power as what is. The poet avoids cliché by refusing to speak directly. Anyone can evoke the signifiers of kitsch, greeting-card signposts that direct us how to feel: overcooked sentiments of loneliness or longing, or conventions of pre-determined emotion. Clement Greenberg was right; kitsch is a kind of fascism of the heart.

But who can sigh like Nick Drake's voice, or like Miles Davis's trumpet? Who can understate enough to convey this subterranean truth? Who dares even to feel in this way—with heroes like these, whose lives were often as tortured as their art is transcendent? There is a certain violence in the willingness of the artist to exchange a peaceable life for immortality. In theory, they should not be mutually exclusive. But so often they seem to be. Nina Simone, at her best, demanding dignity, fearless, it seems, yet often broken-hearted. Billie Holliday, of course. Chopin, somehow evoking in his nocturnes both the transcendence of Romantic beauty and the knowledge of his own transience. Schumann and Schubert as well, in similar keys. Elliot Smith. Sonic Youth, in poetic moments. The Velvet Underground's third album, after the feedback died down, painting the sadness of the outsider. Hasidic *niggunim*, especially from Breslov, and even more especially when set sparingly, on a single flute or clarinet or voice. John Coltrane's "Blue Train" and even, in its way, "A Love Supreme." The Beck of *Sea Change* and *Morning Phase.* Cole Porter, Lauryn Hill, Bon Iver, Joni Mitchell, Radiohead, some of Louis Armstrong, Nusrat Fateh Ali Khan, Debussy, Thelonious Monk—countless others, really, all of whom are alchemists of pain into beauty; but not alchemists, exactly, for in the alchemical art the base metal disappears, whereas in this transformation, its essence is revealed.

I wonder if I met the devil at the crossroads, whether I would sell my soul to make a music which had never been heard before. I hope I would have the courage.

The truthfulness to this music, like the truthfulness of emotional presence, is perhaps the crux of the matter, since whatever God is, It must be closely related to truth. Denial, deception, delusion—these are all in opposition to what is. No amount of resistance can escape the omnipresence of that which is resisted, whether it is the joy of a summer's day or the perfect, brilliant stillness of a winter's late-afternoon dusk. Pushing away the beauty of the latter in favor of an eternal summer is like lying in a tanning bed in the depths of January: It may produce the surface of a symptom of happiness, but only at the cost of truncating the rhythms which, more than any individual occasion, bring about a unity with the fluctuations of nature herself.

Thus, there is a kind of wholeness to this sadness. Unlike despair, which carries with it a story of perpetuity; and unlike self-pity, which whines for what is desired or deserved; a sadness unembellished by the verbiage of desire is pure in its character. Not always simple—there are many notes to it, which is why the chords and melodies of music are so apt a synecdoche, and many variations that defy our language's paucity of synonyms. There is even a new series online called the "Dictionary of Obscure Sorrows," inventing new words for subtle gradations of sadness.

Perhaps, in an age infatuated with dissimulation, this is what holds so much appeal about the honesty of sad music: It is, above all, truthful. The appeal is not necessarily in the marketplace, where meeting the needs of others, rather than expressing the yearnings of oneself, generally succeeds best. The solace is elsewhere.

Nothing is more depressing than the forced happiness of a pep rally. (Kurt Cobain was right too.) Real joy comes about from relaxing the bonds of 'ought' and allowing the bliss of 'is,' and thus allowing the full range of emotion to arise and unfold. For this I often have use of a priest, someone like Joni Mitchell or Elliot Smith to remind me of the terrible beauty that lies where suppositions are suspended and sadness is true. Then I find myself opened to generations of religious geniuses from Gautama Buddha to John of the Cross, to the paradoxes of Nachman of Bratzlav, and to melody itself. It comes through a surrendering-into, an uncovering, an allowing; simply a cessation of the effort of maintaining appearances is enough. I remember again what sleeps in minor keys.

What is the depth of minor-key *niggunim* absent from the relative major? Probably just a quirk of harmonics or culture; different, I am sure, in other parts of the world; but in this time, in this place, evocative of the emptiness inside that reflects the emptiness beyond. Relaxing the constrictions that would force it to take shape, I find the salvation to be real—precisely because it promises nothing, changes nothing, wrestles with nothing, accepts everything.

So there is the resting. But there is also more: the remembered revelation that to be sad is, itself, a flavor of experience that can be appreciated and enjoyed. When the music of sadness plays, and when it is good, it evokes a sensibility the notes of which are subtle and, in a way, delightful. Of course there is pleasure in the wide-open summer days, which linger and are filled with sunshine. But the still, sad music of autumn, so gentle and knowing, so wise, can be a friend as well. This is what we've fought so hard to avoid? This deliciousness?

The resting, then, and the poetry, and the joy; that the enemy is not an enemy, that the shadow is not hateful, that it need not be imagined or transformed into light in order to have a place in redemption. Just the first few notes of Miles Davis' version of "I Fall in Love Too Easily," descending along the E minor seventh chord, in an elegy of breath and legato: It takes so little to be consummated, this union of opposites.

I want to express to you the transformative power this contrary movement has had for me. It is a small thing, really, this redemption of ordinary sadness. But when I am able to catch its advent, and when I am fortunate to have the time to accommodate it, what might previously have led to a spiral of fruitless soul-searching and desperate efforts to change what has naturally come to pass is instead an occasion for a quiet celebration. A glass of wine and the right music are neither striking cultural innovations nor the usual tools of spirituality (though they do strikingly resemble the objects of religious ritual) yet there is a privacy and an intimacy to our inner ranges of sadness that makes them almost secret. Another honesty, then, to unfold. I would let this be my communion, my *kiddush*: the sanctification of the ordinarily despised, the blessing of a heart no longer in search of its mending.

In a sense, the redemption of sadness is the truth of truthfulness itself. Merely the absence of deceit is itself a source of joy. It is a miracle, I think, that it is so: that the truth sets one free. But not the truth, exactly—rather, the truthfulness, the clarity of the glass through which one is able to see. That very clearness of vision, more than what is perceived, is itself the liberation that is sought.

The Blues, Prayer and Unrequited Love

"The Blues ain't about making yourself feel better," said Bleeding Gums Murphy to Lisa Simpson. "It's about making other people feel worse."

The method of the Blues is that by using a common, conventional language (love, whiskey, crossroads), the essence of sorrow is communicated without the distractions of specificity. I don't really care, after all, what you think about mortgages or medical care; but I do care what you feel about them, because maybe I feel it too. And by listening to you sigh the way I do, maybe there's a moment of communion that can happen, an instant of empathy that will remind me that I'm not alone in being alone, that in fact, aloneness is the only thing we all share. And in that communication, connection. It feels good to feel bad when someone else feels bad too.

And so the Blues uses a common, almost meaningless language to convey the universality of feeling, abstracted from the particulars of experience, yet grounded in the archetypes of America.

And the experience is immediate; the expression is real in the moment of its expressing. There's a kind of mysticism to it, because the conventional words gesture beyond themselves—a mystery conveyed in what cannot be transcribed or translated, the inflection of the voice, the pull of the melody. To sing in this way, you must be naked in the music and expiate the pain in song.

Bleeding Gums is right that the blues is about making other people feel worse, but only because feeling worse is feeling better; because feeling worse is feeling real; because feeling worse is the only way out, because the only way out is through. It feels good to feel bad sometimes.

I remember, at the end of a three year relationship, the way the winter unfolded, long, and cold, and lonely, and often darker than the deepest sea, to quote Nick Drake, a valued companion at the time. I felt at times thrown back into spiritual grade school, learning the basics all over again. Sadness, suffering, acceptance, brokenness, adequacy, loss.

"You're at your best when you're most connected," one of my meditation teachers once told me, "and you're at your most connected when you allow yourself to be sad."

"Is he dark enough to see your light?" asked Damien Rice, in my 'breakup album' from that year.

I worked on the basics. Letting the mind stop desiring, for one moment at a time, for this feeling in the heart to be anything other than it is. Letting the emptiness be full. Letting the sadness happen. It felt great when it unfolded on its own, great and awful and human and real. *This is actually happening*, I felt.

The language of prayer is similar to the language of the blues. It's cliché when it's theology, but when the heart is broken, it gestures toward something profound, right from within its preposterous convention.

I don't mean here the self-transcendence of ecstasy, those moments of glorious drumming and dancing and singing and pounding, in which the heart leaps out of its confines. I mean the second-person language of yearning, pining, wanting, needing. Robert Johnson, John Lee Hooker. Searching, not finding; desiring, not consummating. This yearning love, the Sufis say, is the very last of our tools to be set down on the path to oneness—the very last. Sometimes I reach out, and nothing reaches back.

And yet there is beauty in reaching out. I want to love. I prefer to love; I prefer to love even if I will not be loved back, even if doing so aches in the heart and embarrasses me. Even if it takes away my dignity, I don't care; this is how I want to be in human affairs, and so in divine ones also.

On a meditation retreat that same winter, I remember, when Friday night came along, that I felt grateful for the break. But when it came time for Kabbalat Shabbat, I was stuck with doubt. *What am I doing this for*, I asked myself. Finally, I gave up; it made no sense.

And then the gates opened. As soon as I stopped expecting anything, stopped wanting anything, I was set free to do what the heart really wanted, which was to offer and express love and gratitude and desire and joy. I didn't have an ecstatic prayer experience. But I did have a sense of communion, if only with myself, and the honesty of my wanting to express love. That is what I really wanted: to hear my heart. Not God's—mine.

Like the Blues, the words were basically irrelevant. But the irrelevance was part of the point. Nothing could express how I was feeling, not without cliché. Better to have words that came from outside, which I could speak without adopting, without committing—just speaking, singing, bowing, swaying. Like the Blues, these forms captured the formless.

It felt good to feel worse.

I Know a Place Where There's Still Something Going On

John Lennon said in 1965, "You don't have to hear what Bob Dylan sings, you just have to hear how he sings it."

To those who can't stand Dylan's various singing voices (there have been several iterations, over his fifty-year career), this may seem like an odd observation. A lot of Dylan's casual listeners fish the words out of the melody, appreciating them despite the nasal, guttural, and sometimes barely intelligible delivery.

But then there are us fans. And to us, Dylan's delivery is part of the point. The fierceness of *It's Alright Ma (I'm Only Bleeding)*, the brokenness of *You're a Big Girl Now*, the old age of *When the Deal Goes Down*. These moods are in the music and lyrics, yes, but they are carried by the singing. Lennon was right.

In his most recent work, the expressiveness of Dylan's singing has taken a central role, as his writing has tended more toward the generalities of the blues than to the verbal artistry that marked the first and second phases of his career. He's even made an album of covers, wherein the words are signifiers not of their specific referents, but of the emotional content beneath them. Like the blues, they use a language of convention to express that which is cheapened when it is communicated directly.

Really, it has been this way for decades. The snarl of the hipster period (1965-66) the musicality of the basement tapes, and, for that matter, the confused vacuity of some of his least music (1981-89)—in all these cases, the singing, not the words, is the primary gesture toward meaning. There is often not a verbal explication of this meaning—an effort which frequently ends in bathos. It is breathed into the words.

At first, the brokenness in Dylan was outside: injustice, hypocrisy. Later, it moved inward: heartbreak (*Blood on the Tracks*) mortality (*Time Out of Mind*). I'm grateful that I'm old enough to remember the age of albums, and the way we used to play them all the way through. The sadness in *Blood on the Tracks*, recorded as Dylan was in the midst of a divorce from his wife Sara (of "Sad-Eyed Lady of the Lowlands" fame), is almost palpable, even though the songs are free of the ridiculous white-boy whining that has subsequently become ubiquitous in guitar pop. He sings these words directly, without a lot of ornamentation, and something about that straightforward delivery enables the deliciously heartbreaking pain in the music and lyrics to shine.

When I first heard the album, I was a closeted teenager, a would-be poet who was teased at school and home on Friday nights. That's a far remove from a 35-year-old celebrity on the eve of his first divorce. Really, I shouldn't have been able to relate to any of what Dylan was saying. But because of that delivery, and because of the universal movements of heart that lay underneath the particularities of his situation, I felt like I had a companion in my loneliness. I could feel the wistfulness in "Shelter from the Storm," even though Dylan was singing about losing something I had yet to experience. I was too young to have known the regret in "Simple Twist of Fate," but not too young to know the sense of loss, absence, sadness.

I know that for most people who have heard of him, Dylan is synonymous with a very different set of songs—generation-defining protests of injustice, plugged-in word salads that announced a new consciousness. But for me, the resonance lies in quieter places, which is one reason I've loved the last two decades of grizzled Americana and take-no-prisoners Old Testament justice. He's singing about real things, and his now-ravaged voice has the credibility to speak with authority.

And when Dylan has found transcendence, it has been in the expressive capacity of music itself. Summer days are gone, he sings in one recent track, but I know a place where there's still something going on. Youth is past, mortality looms, the world has evil in it, the individual is in pain—but in the poetry of sadness itself, growled or plucked or crunched with the band, is redemption, even a kind of immortality.

Spoken Lonesomeness is Prophecy

> I'm an old man now,
> and a lonesome man in Kansas,
> but not afraid to speak my lonesomeness...
> because it's not only my lonesomeness,
> it's ours, all over America, O tender fellows,
> and spoken lonesomeness is prophecy.
>
> Allen Ginsberg, "Wichita Vortex Sutra Part 3"

When I was younger, and just starting out on the spiritual path, I would look at the sad and lonely people on retreat with me and say "I'm not like them—I'm here for God, not because my life is so pathetic that I need to fill the hole." I can take care of myself fine, thank you; I'm here for mysticism.

Thankfully, that arrogance didn't last long. I thought spirituality was going to be about angels and visions, but it turned out to be about honesty, clear seeing, and all the pain the angels were meant to help me avoid. The more spiritual work I did—Buddhist meditation retreats, shamanic rituals, ecstatic Jewish prayer—the more I chipped away at the false layers of ego surrounding a core of pain, loneliness, and suffering. I started to understand why the first of the Buddha's noble truths is that suffering exists.

And yet, all in all, I've had it pretty good: born a middle-class white male in the richest country in history, to parents who loved me as best they could, and with uncountable privileges of education, background, and community. But, like many gay men of a certain age and above, I also spent two decades hating myself, wishing I were different, longing for a life I could never have, and not understanding who I was, how I loved, or how I was wounding myself by wishing I was otherwise. And like almost everyone, I've experienced my share of loss over the years.

But most of all, I think it was love, and its lack, that first impelled my spiritual work. Is it coincidence that while I pined for love that I could never consummate, I also yearned for the love of a somewhat distant and judgmental God, whom I feared as much as loved? I had many spiritual experiences during those years, but they were almost always tinged with authority and conditionality. I rejoiced in the sacred spaces of religion, but there was always a need to impress this distant God, to do the right thing so I would merit his love.

I don't regret my loneliness. It stays with me, even now when my life is so different, both as a kind of emotional ballast, and as an opening. With it, I am connected to my own truth, history, and soul; I am at my least arrogant; my most open to others. What do I know, then? Nothing new, and nothing special: just impermanence and relinquishment. I have seen how each of us is existentially alone, and reaching outward or inward to fill the emptiness. When, almost paradoxically, it takes on the character of fullness precisely when it is left alone and empty.

I think a love that is forever is a love that is forever renewed. When one person says to another, "I will love you forever," it would be naïve to think that the present experience of love, whatever it is, will endure forever—or that the person whom we love will be the same years from now. Neither the love nor the lover will remain so constant, because everyone is constantly changing. Thus the experience of love changes, its character shifts; hopefully it deepens, as I have been blessed to experience. "For better or for worse" is not "I will love you forever as I love you right now," but rather "I will renew my love for you forever, in different forms, in different modes, as a constantly renewing act of devotion."

I learned this, I think, from my loneliness. Healing from the pain of a broken relationship showed me how I was still turning outward for completion, instead of inward for wholeness—or rather, the wholeness of brokenness. Shamanic work, plumbing the depths of my physical and spiritual being in the sacred valley of Peru, convinced me, finally, that my purpose on this planet is not to write books, to make money teaching law, or even to change the world, but simply to love—to accept all of it, including the pain, and let the acceptance melt into freedom. And many years of insight meditation has shown me how it is tragic to hold onto any state of mind, to mistake it for a permanent self—and how liberating it is to let go. Love and let go, love and let go. Was it so complicated? No, I'm a slow learner.

And surely it is not a coincidence that now my God loves more than judges, and is always there, without fanfare or faith, or the fireworks of interesting mindstates, simply when I let go, and continue to fall, past ego and identity and the sense of existence itself. I have prayed in caves and at shrines, writhed in energetic ecstasy, drunk the soma of South America, and experienced profound states of bliss and equanimity and holiness and pain. I have known Being intimately and directly, dispassionately and passionately, in emptiness and in fullness. Spiritual practice has even taught me how joy and sadness can coexist, if only the resistance to sadness is relinquished; such a surrender dissolves loneliness into pure aloneness, the simple freedom of Being itself. And it is tinged with tears and love.

I am blessed to be on this karmic ride which I did not ordain and certainly did not intend. And throughout, I have been impelled by loneliness. Would I have learned the deeper lessons of love if I had not been lonely myself? Would I have taken the time to sit in silence for weeks, months at a time if my heart had not been broken? Would I have made the time, if the alternative were life with a partner? Would I even have cared? And if I had not, would I have opened my heart to love, from within and without, in the way that I do now? Or would love have remained a private sort of matter, a part of life, but not its essence?

From one perspective of a householder, my spiritual work might look like a "substitute for love" (Madonna, of course); like consolation, or delusion, or a kind of therapy that, if it works, will allow me to be well-adjusted. Well, good for me. I think that from the perspective of a spiritual practitioner, suffering is a gateway to wisdom, not something to be abolished.

During one recent meditation retreat, I entered a state of absorbed concentration in which the powers of visualization become greatly enhanced; with enough concentration, you can create your own perceptual universe, which can be of great use for insight into the self. (My assumption is that such spaces are entirely mind-created, but the experiences of absorption conform to the descriptions of mystical states found in Western literature. They are also the holiest places I have ever been.) During one such experience, I met with the spirit and vision of Allen Ginsberg, warm and benevolent, pleased with my Jewish Dharma journey, and perhaps doing me the visionary favor that William Blake had done him half a century ago, in a Morningside Heights apartment. I had been very lonely that morning, remembering wounds from childhood and relationship and beyond, and so I asked him if I would ever be healed.

Smiling warmly, he said no, there is only "great pain, and great love." I think this is sufficient.

Rilke

The poetry of Rilke is a treasure that its lovers often find on their own. In an earlier time, we'd discover it in a used bookstore, stumbling on it in surprise and in unexpected solidarity. There is someone who feels as we feel, and who has captured sacred loneliness, the heartbreaking beauty of the heart alone, in words more pure than we had thought possible. I miss the possibility of such discoveries.

But even today, Rilke's poems, particularly those on religious themes, often speak of solitude, from solitude, to solitude—and as such, provide companionship in aloneness. His is a voice calling out to a God who inhabits solitary spaces.

> I'm too alone in the world, yet not alone enough
> To make each hour holy.
> I'm too small in the world, yet not small enough
> To be simply in your presence, like a thing—
> Just as it is.

This poem—Book of Hours, I.13—is part of Rilke's "Book of a Monastic Life," but Rilke was not an actual monk like Ryokan.

Like most of us who imagine ourselves to be contemplatives, he lives in the world, and, at least in part, of it. He exists somewhere in between the hermitage and the theater. Solitude, even loneliness, seems like the necessary condition for a monastic sensibility to arise in such a context. One has to be alone enough to make each hour holy.

Yet Rilke is not alone enough; he is not a monk; he feels only intimations; he is still, like most of us, pulled by the sounds and sights of life in the world.

In another poem from the same collection, which I quoted at the beginning of this part (for these renditions, I've based my own translations on those of Joanna Macy & Anita Barrows, Robert Bly, and A.S. Kline, and on the original poems), Rilke suggests a middle space between renunciation and engagement: the company of the wise, or those who know secret things. But if that is not possible, Rilke says, aloneness is preferable to the small talk of parties and lunches. Solitude and silence are gifts, not privations. They provide the interludes Rilke speaks of in another poem from the Book of Hours, I.5:

> I love the dark hours of my being.
> My mind deepens into them.
> There I can find, as in old letters,
> The days of my life, already lived,
> And held like a legend, and understood.
> Then the knowing comes: I can open
> To another life that's wide and timeless.

There is, for some of us at least, something to be loved about the dark hours—not just accepted, learned from, and merged into, but actually loved. They are fertile times, as Rilke writes here. The dark hours are portals to the timeless, as if the light occludes it. They open to the wide and timeless, precisely in their emptiness.

They are, as in this excerpt from the Tenth Duino elegy, beloved; they ought not be squandered; the nights of anguish are nights of revelation:

> How dear you will be to me, then, nights
> of anguish. Inconsolable sisters, why did I not
> kneel more to greet you, lose myself more
> in your loosened hair? How we squander our hours of pain.
> How we gaze beyond them into the bitter duration,
> to see if they have an end. Though they are nothing but
> our winter foliage, our dark evergreen,
> one of the seasons of our inner year—not only
> season—but place, settlement, camp, soil, dwelling.

Rothko

A few years ago, I visited the Rothko Chapel in Houston. In many ways, the chapel is an anomaly: a modern tomb amid high-end homes, a liberal center for human rights in the Lone Star State, and a fierce, uncompromising installation of vast, mostly black Rothko paintings that challenges the tourists who visit it.

I've long loved Rothko, whose spiritual sadness is a visual expression of the unification of sorrow and joy. Like the musicality of music itself, his abstract expressionism dispenses with figuration entirely. It is emotion unelaborated, without exemplification. I can sit and become absorbed in some of his work and forget that time is passing.

In Houston, I was struck by the chapel's juxtaposition of Rothko's art with the human rights mission. It seemed to me that The Rothko Chapel is the antithesis of kitsch, and as such, is essentially progressive. Bad conservative architecture (like the World War II memorial in Washington, D.C., for example) demands that you feel a certain way; stimulus, response. It is (Clement Greenberg again) authoritarian in this way. You Will Feel This.

Rothko evokes, rather than commands. Stare at his tricolor paintings and see what arises. In my experience, they have very definite resonances—perhaps I'm making it all up, but it seems to me a form of communication without signification. It's as if his tortured spirit is in the room with me, at once terribly sad and awfully beautiful. Without wanting to seem melodramatic, I sometimes find it almost too much to bear.

Kitsch believes in simple answers and simpler sentiments. Cliché, patriotism, the implied, tyrannical universality of common sense. Art such as Rothko's confounds certain conventional notions—once, when I was rapt with attention at a Rothko, someone walked by and made the usual comment that "my kid could do that"—and transcends clichéd signifiers to directly convey the beauty of the shadow.

The progressive values of the Rothko Chapel resonate, then, with the kind of contemplation that Rothko's work invites.

There are no hymnals; only silence, before these vast blacknesses. Directed sentiments are not foisted upon the visitor.

And at the same time, there is a common humanity that the paintings evoke. You, too, can feel this. Perhaps you can even learn to evoke it. We are human, and this is beautiful—at once shared and unique to each individual. The experience of another is not knowable to me, yet I can feel in solidarity with them. Particular boundaries define identity, and can be transcended, if the programmatic is restrained in the name of the spacious.

The silence gloriously aches.

Northern Sound

Each sound I hear is music, and when I experience it that way, which takes a certain amount of intention, there is a kind of alchemy that transmutes sadness into its simultaneous joy.

I've experienced John Cage's 4'33" live a handful of times— it's often mistitled "four minutes and thirty three seconds of silence," but it's not silence, of course; it's comprised of the sounds that one can hear in the given interval. The ritualization of the piece—performers, exact timing—seems essential. It creates a gateway, or an arch. It sets parameters, as if framing the sky in a work of James Turrell. It says, listen in here for music.

And then what is within, is music. Music doesn't depend upon pleasant melodies. It is rather the attitude of attention that transforms sound into art.

If not John Cage, then George Harrison, "If you're listening to this song/You might think the chords are going wrong/But they're not./I just wrote it like that." Once again: It's not that the chords are wrong simply because they defy expectation or hope. They are what they are.

I might paraphrase it: If you're listening to yourself, you might think the heart is going wrong. But it's not. It's just unfolding like that.

Both Cage and Harrison were dedicated contemplative practitioners—Cage a Zen Buddhist, Harrison eventually a Krishna devotee. Both were forthright about the connection between their spiritual work and their very different artistic outputs. Cage was interested in chance, spontaneity, moments of full emptiness. Harrison was more colorful: in *My Sweet Lord*, full of devotion and love; the sadness of *Isn't It A Pity*, the mysticism of *Within You Without You*. Sometimes it's the transparency and acceptance of *Only a Northern Song*. (At times, unfortunately, it's pedantic, like *It Is He (Jai Sri Krishna)* , which is perhaps less convincing.) Sometimes, as in *Wonderwall Music*, conventional musical notes drop away, and one is left with a sound that precedes music, but is music. Harrison almost approaches Cage at such times.

At a certain point, 'spirituality' itself drops away as a meaningful definer of experience. If someone laughs or coughs during *4'33"*, is my "spiritual vibe" disturbed? Is my spirituality too precious for what actually happens?

As that answer turns to the negative, as the attitude of attention extends beyond the opening and closing of the piano top, it becomes harder to define its subject—both in the sense of attention, and that of delimitation. It's as if the piano is always open, if I am. Which sometimes I am.

No One Makes Mistakes

Not too long ago, I made a mistake that had severe consequences. I'm ashamed of the details, too ashamed to recall them here. And anyway the details seem less important than what my mistake had in common with the errors we all make from time to time: It was a combination of bad luck and bad judgment that led to humiliation, regret, and loss.

All of us have screwed up now and then, on large stages or small ones. This should bring us comfort, but generally it doesn't.

For weeks after the incident, I vacillated between extremes of blaming myself and blaming others. This was easy to do, since what transpired was indeed partly my fault and partly the fault of other people. But rather than hold the two sides in balance, I tended to lurch from one to the other: Either this was all me, or all him, either I'm horrible or he is.

For a while, as long as the majority of blame lay on the other person, I was okay. I felt angry and strong. I had made a small mistake, yes, but *he* was selfish, vain, insecure, and worse. The narrative I adopted didn't get me off the hook, but it was essentially the story of being a victim. And it was the version I shared with most other people.

The Gate of Tears

But it didn't work over the long term. Maybe for some, a self-deception repeated often enough becomes a kind of truth. Truthfully, I would've been happy for that to happen to me; I'm not so proud of my integrity. But that didn't happen. Weeks upon weeks of repeating this story didn't lift my mood, and obviously it didn't make the situation any different.

There were good days and bad days. On good days, I moved on, focused on other things, and only remembered the trauma of the event once or twice. On bad days, though, the enormity of what I had lost (or had taken from me) as a result of this mistake seemed unbearable. I felt intensities of sadness that I had not experienced in years. It often felt violent.

On one of those bad days, I gave up trying to make anything better. Although I knew that responsibility for what had happened was shared, I took all the blame myself—but for real this time, not in some self-flagellating way. Suppose it was all my fault. Suppose I brought this mess upon myself—that it really was just because of me. What then?

With the attempt to justify set down, some insight arose. I made this bad decision because I was in a difficult period in my life: There was an illness in the family, and I was exhausted, and I was needy. I thought that no one would find out—was sure, actually, though of course I was wrong. And maybe my judgment wasn't so good anyway.

None of these facts are meant as excuses. On the contrary: I didn't want to excuse anything, but to understand—or at least see—as many of the causes of my mistake as I could. Nor did I have any auto-pedagogical aim in mind. I wasn't trying to avoid making the same mistake in the future. I really was curious: What had happened?

As each of the causes and conditions became clearer, the sense of rage decreased. The whole incident began to seem almost mechanical. These causes were present, these effects followed. There was no ego involved, no "I" to praise, blame, or excuse for its actions. There was a human being, with assorted strengths and weaknesses, in an extreme situation, who made a bad decision and unexpectedly got caught. And, yes, there was another human being who then reacted in a destructive way. But nowhere, in me or him, was there some independent agency that might be blamed. It's not like there was the sum of all causes and conditions of the universe… and then me. It was like clockwork.

Causes and effects are all that's out there—and they're all empty of substance. A cause leads to an effect, whether trivial or grave. In more explicit, Buddhist terminology, there is simply dependent origination and non-self: One thing leads to another. And, of course, we react, with suffering, or acceptance, or rage, or whatever. In my case, there were causes, effects, and sadness.

From the beginning of this period of crisis, my close friends advised me to have compassion for myself. This was a tough situation, and whoever is to blame for it, what's important is to treat myself gently and try to heal. But that hadn't stuck. After all, if this was my fault, I don't deserve compassion! Maybe that's why I focused on blaming the other person.

Once I saw, felt, and believed that this almost tragic set of circumstances was empty of blame for anyone, suddenly I felt compassion for the whole conundrum. Him, me, the people caught in the middle, the work that we could've done but didn't, the personal costs I paid and continue to pay—all of it. Even now, the sense of compassion predominates. What a sad mess. It's really too bad that it happened.

Again, no excuses. On the contrary, this insight into the whole conundrum came only when I stopped making excuses and allowed the worst case scenario—that this was a result of my actions—to be the case. Rather, there is a peacefulness intrinsic to seeing the mess more clearly. This happened because of causes, it in turn caused worse things to happen, suffering all around, compassion.

Impermanence

When loneliness arises, it often carries with it the illusion of permanence. The transitory experience of loneliness is hard, but the thought that it will never pass is torture. When we know that a separation is temporary, the longing for reunion is often sweet, tinged as it is with love. But when a separation is thought to be permanent, then its timbre changes to one of bitterness, lamentation, or even despair.

Some partings are indeed permanent: those occasioned by death most obviously. Yet even then, the *experience* of separation is impermanent. Impermanence is a feature of every conditioned phenomenon, even mountains and stars—*a fortiori* the movements of the heart, which arise and pass very quickly when they are not propped up by the mind.

The physical impermanence of mountains does not help us much. Yes, over the course of millions of years, the mountain will change. But you and I will disintegrate long before the mountain will. So what is the relevance of its impermanence to us?

This: When the mind has turned its attention to the moment-to-moment phenomena of experience, mountains become radically impermanent, changing in perception from one fraction of a second to the next. Though the mountain itself may endure for aeons, the perception of seeing the mountain is interrupted by sounds, the weight of the body, the sensation of movement in the legs. The emotional tone associated with it shifts constantly, from interest to boredom to awe to delight.

In this way, the emotional experience of a mountain (or a person, or a situation in which we find ourselves) shifts a hundred times over the span of just a few minutes. And, like the frames of a film, these apparently continuous perceptions are, in fact, comprised of countless momentary particles of thinking, feeling, judgment. Really, there are three kinds of impermanence: the mundane truth that eventually, everything passes away; the somewhat more refined understanding of the shifting nature of our experience, even of effectively constant phenomena; and third, the extremely subtle impermanence of perception itself.

These points are of more than neurological interest. When encountered directly, especially during meditation, the truth of impermanence brings about liberation, and can transform the experience of sadness, pain, anger, or any other supposedly undesirable state of mind.

The first form of impermanence is, as has already been suggested, the least helpful, even if it is the easiest to see. Often, I find it to be no consolation at all. But the other two I have found, over the years, to be profound. On meditation retreats, I have watched the mind glide effortlessly from ecstasy to apathy to loneliness to nervousness to peace to a sense of mystical unity to sadness to planning—all within a few minutes. Outside of retreats, I have been astonished to see that similar changes in mood happen just as quickly, only beneath my regular notice. What is there to hold onto, for better or for worse, when the heart moves so quickly? These stories of solitude or sadness—and also dreams of eternal bliss—are undermined with just a few moments' attention.

The third form of impermanence has been equally powerful. No matter how strong the state of mind, whether positive or negative, it can be interrupted and interspersed with other perceptions. In fact, it already is being interrupted; the only question is whether I choose to pay attention to the reality of experience or construct a false solidity out of one or more elements of it. The life of the human mind is a manic channel-surfing of perceptions, feelings, thoughts, and mental formations. Try it right now; try to actually follow the chain of perception, rather than focus on any one thing. Reading, pressure on the sit-bones, interest, boredom, curiosity, thoughts of other people, breathing in, to-do list, seeing the page, the weight of the book, breathing out, a smile, lust, a sense of hunger or fullness—life is not so continuous as it seems.

Despair is a phenomenon of burrowing into a single mental object, and staying there. It ignores the truth that all objects, mental or physical, are constantly being interrupted by other ones. It chooses one *idee fixe*, one obsession, and digs into it, sinks into it. This is as unhelpful as it is inaccurate—not only when the mind burrows into a negative emotion, but even when it digs into a positive one. How many times have I felt some joy, with a lover or during spiritual practice or after achieving some goal, and thought, absurdly, that this joy would never pass, that the ecstasy would go on forever? Now I've got it! Now I'm enlightened! Now I don't need anything! Now I am content! And yet, all things pass, states of mind faster than most. Maybe if I'd paid more attention to the word "now," I might've hurt less when the conditions shifted.

Seeing how even the most exuberant or unhappy mindstates are constantly being interrupted by other perceptions leads to a kind of mental balance. One need not even remember that "this too shall pass," because mindfulness is strong, it is already arising and passing, arising and passing, over and over again.

I used to find these aspects of impermanence to be like ants at the picnic of joy, ruining everything with their *memento mori*. At some point over the last few years, however, my relationship to impermanence shifted—and now I experience it as comfort. What changed? I got hurt, I healed, I had peak experiences followed by valleys of shadow, I held on to a love affair that lasted past its prime. Life happened.

I still am blessed by, and enjoy, glorious peak experiences: love, spiritual communions, ecstatic moments of self-transcendence, deep encounters with other people. But I have grown a little more suspicious of them, and a little less impressed by the ups and downs. I actually find it more joyful to hear the voice that reminds me: "Love and let go, it's going to pass, and in fact it's passing already."

This may sound like even more of a downer, but I experience this voice as one of love. It protects me; it gently holds my heart, protecting it from wounding itself in an excess of enthusiasm or hopelessness. It's part of how I understand the process of getting older. The oscillations of the soul are part of its nature; they teach me the truth and, I find, this kind of truth sets me free.

Depression

Throughout this book, I have tried to maintain the distinction between the ordinary pain that is part of human life—sadness, loss, grief, loneliness—and depression. I want to explain why I have done this and what I mean.

The main reason is that I am not a doctor and do not have training as a mental health professional. I have counseled many people over the years who have been diagnosed with forms of depression or depressive disorder, as well as many who have not, and many about whom I have wondered. But I have never dispensed medical advice, and I am not a psychiatrist or psychologist. Depression is a serious illness, reflecting (we think) an imbalance of chemicals in the brain. It can lead to the loss of the ability to live one's life, even to carry out the basic functions of living. Unlike sadness, depression should be addressed and treated—the opposite of the allowing, co-existing, and letting-be that is characteristic of the gate of tears.

I also think, based on personal experience, that ordinary sadness and depression are two different things. Clearly, the lines between these conditions of mind are blurry, yet in my personal experience, I can tell the difference. I have occasionally suffered from depression, and occasionally taken low doses of SSRI's to counteract it. In my case (though not in others), these periods have had external prompts: breakups, deaths, illness. To be sure, prompts are not the same as causes; based on my family history, I assume the causes to be a mix of genetics and environment. But these difficult periods were occasioned by something, and gradually lifted as time went on.

During these times, the feeling-tone of depression was clearly distinct from that of ordinary sadness. Depression is not really a mood that comes and goes; it is a continual condition. Physically, there is a weightiness in the chest that is almost constant. Emotionally, there is a sluggishness and a greyness of mind. The clouds occasionally part—often as a result of the practices I describe in this book, other times because of external stimuli—but they come back. It is less a blackness than a weighty, overcast gray.

Again, in my experience, this state of mind is less transitory and more pervasive than that of occasional sadness. In my life, it eventually, gradually lifts, but this is more a matter of months than of moments. When I coexist with sadness, it passes (even if it later returns). Without resistance, the feeling simply is, and it eventually goes of its own accord. Not so with depression. When I have been depressed, it is as if every feeling—joy, love, sadness—is dimmed, rendered almost hypothetical in nature. I mimic joy more than I experience it. Nothing good sticks; everything seems worthless.

In my experience of it, then, depression isn't a state of mind; it's a condition that affects all states of mind. I grow short-tempered and irritable. I am much less resilient, on the verge of tears at the slightest provocation. It's not that a new mood is added; rather, every mood is affected. Sadness, grief, joy, and even anger are all part of life, and deserve to be experienced. Depression blocks them.

Fortunately, the periods of depression that I have experienced have been just that—periods. Many people who suffer from depression are not so fortunate, and find their depression resistant to medications, therapies, and all their best efforts. I am also a high-functioning depressive. I usually still work, still go out, still talk. I know from friends and from books like Andrew Solomon's *The Noonday Demon* that others are not so lucky. Depression can be thoroughly debilitating, and life-threatening. I have had friends end their lives because of it.

We all have our opinions about the medicalization of depression, the over-prescription of medication, and the cavalier way in which some people may pop pills like candy. There are certainly excesses. But I am equally certain that anti-depressants help people, and that the stigma around depression (and other mental illness) prevents many people from getting the help they need. Given the choice, I would rather have depression over-treated than under-treated.

I have worried, at times, that some readers of *The Gate of Tears* might use it as a way to self-medicate their mental illness with spirituality. I think that I've seen this among some of my students. At such times, I feel like a charlatan. I want to emphasize that, yes, sadness is beautiful and can coexist with joy. *And* depression ought to be treated.

How to know which is which? I am not sure there is any single heuristic that applies to everyone. Many clinicians focus on behavior: Is this getting in the way of your life? Are you able to live the life you want to live? Others focus on phenomenology: Are you ever suicidal? Do you have trouble experiencing joy? These seem like good places to start.

Others still, such as the authors of the book *The Loss of Sadness*, emphasize context. They point out that it's perfectly normal to feel sad after a loss or difficult transition, and "normal" is the exact opposite of a disorder. So, for them, depression is "sadness that is caused by a harmful dysfunction of loss-response mechanisms." Dyfunction, not function; sadness itself is not a disorder.

One time, several years ago, I sank into a depressive period that lasted throughout the winter. I wondered whether I should restart medication, or whether I might continue the practices in this book instead. I found that I could, indeed, "be with" the periods of darkness that were frequently arising.

But it was almost all I was doing. My life was like one of those painful meditation periods that I described earlier, where all that's going on is a certain pain, and you sit with it, and sit with it, and at some point, you stop learning from it. I wasn't learning from this greyness anymore; I was just putting up with it, telling myself that I was being a good Buddhist by doing so (a screw-up Buddhists call "attachment to views" and "attachment to self"). Who knows, maybe I could have sat with the depression longer, and give myself some kind of award. But the wiser voice inside me said that it was time for an antidote. I went to see my doctor. I don't regret that decision.

You Again

Among my weaknesses: I am what Buddhist psychology would call a "greed type." I want it all, and don't want to choose. I've had several careers, several spiritual paths, and several areas of scholarly focus. I am fully aware that it's impossible to be really good at more than one or two things, but I keep doing a lot of things.

One of my persistent both-ands is spirituality and success. Liberation, enlightenment, compassion, wisdom, love—yes, please. And/But also success, fame, money, respect, accomplishment, achievement, impactful activism, a kind of immortality. I am pretty sure that the two are mutually exclusive, though who knows.

Meanwhile, the drive for success has tainted almost all of the successes that I have enjoyed. I am pretty sure I'm not alone in that.

What has helped has been to notice the drive for what it is. It's impersonal; it's a drive. Humans are hard-wired to develop egos, to be dissatisfied, to strive at various points in our lives. Those who didn't want to advance themselves did not reproduce. It is entirely natural to want—just as it is entirely natural to suffer. And this human, in particular, born into a certain socio-economic group, with various privileges and cultural traits, channels that natural drive in specific, culturally constructed ways. The drive is both nature and nurture; with elements that are inborn and others that are socially constructed. It comes and goes, waxes and wanes.

On good days, I neither fight nor believe the desire. Maybe I listen to it or maybe I don't, but mostly I relax out of it by seeing it for what it is. Oh, you again. Oh, and there's the sense of lack, of insufficiency, of envy, that you carry along with you. I know you well. Let's see if I can hold you without either pushing you out of my mind, or believing anything you have to say. You again.

The drive to achieve may be natural, important, wholesome—or destructive, acquisitive, and shot through with craving. Or all of the above, maybe at different times.

And yet, because I don't want to give it up, I think it's possible to act on this drive for success without making it one's master. Maybe.

Despair

Sadness is not the same as despair. Despair involves time: It will never get better, there is no hope, there is no point to continuing, there is only more pain ahead. Sadness, grief, loss, loneliness, pain—these are present-moment experiences.

Once the stories are released, the fullness of the present remains, with a kind of beauty to it. The key is to not desire anything at all, not seek anything at all. As the Zen teacher Genpo Roshi sometimes says, reside in the "non-seeking, non-desiring mind."

The heart still feels; it may be broken. But it simply *is*.

Theoretically, anger, like sadness, should be accepted for what it is. I've struggled with this, however, since even the energy of anger can be hard to be with, in oneself or especially in another person. Here is where I have gotten so far.

Acting on anger is subtle. On inspection, it reveals itself to be a form of erasure: The expression of anger contains the wish that it dissipate. It is an attempt to change it by converting it into something else. "If I throw this book across the room, I will feel better... dammit." This is not accepting anger; it is trying to be rid of it through action.

Repression is similar. It, too, seeks to dispel anger, this time by pretending it isn't there, squashing it down, stifling it. Sometimes, this is exactly what is required in a given situation. Repeated over time, though, it seems like a bad idea.

So what lies in the space between expression and repression? Seeing, being-with, accommodating, noticing, accepting—somehow (Shinzen Young again) loving it to death. But it's hard to just "see" anger, hatred, and other strong negative mind-states. Theoretically, we should all be able to sit with our negative emotions and notice them and love them in all their fullness, since they are expressions of God, or just of how things are. But that doesn't mean we can all do it. I certainly can't. I'd like to say that I can, but I can't.

Some of my activist friends insist that anger is a helpful motivator. Righteous indignation, they say. If you're not angry, you're not paying attention. But this has also not been my experience.

When I'm angry about something, I'm not articulate in explaining it, and I'm not skillful in opposing it. So much for being a writer or an activist, then. Anyway, I don't find I need to look for reasons to be angry; the newspaper takes care of that. It's not as if I lack for inspiration.

What, then? If not acting out, repressing, or even sublimating anger—is there no alternative to being tossed by it, like a boat on a choppy day?

At my best, the wind blows in, and blows out. The anger rises, but as it's noticed, it doesn't grow—I don't feed it with stories of injustice, self-justification, or wallowing. I drop the narrative, and instead try to get in touch with the pain that's underneath the anger—I'd much rather be sad than be angry. I just sit with it; the energy is what it is.

Would I be more enlightened if I didn't get angry? I have no idea. I feel sure, though, that I would not be more enlightened if I pretended it never happened.

Doubt

Religious traditions aren't fond of doubt. For obvious reasons, you might say—the last thing an authority figure wants is a flock that doubts his (and it is usually his) word.

Doubt can be useful at times, useless at others. Useful, healthy doubt helps to sift truth from falsehood. Useless, unhealthy doubt is the kind that erodes our better natures and wears us down into a cold, cynical core; it is the doubt that lies.

Personally, I prefer even loneliness to doubt. The pain of a lover's departure is nothing compared with the pain of wondering whether we were ever loved at all—or whether it was all delusion all along.

Or consider the doubt of one's own worldview: the sense that the selfish, materialistic, "practical" men really have it right, and that we are only acting out psychic trauma or dysfunction.

Or consider how a mere passing hunger or thirst can make all our art and love seem purposeless, even annoying.

But if sadness teaches compassion, doubt teaches patience. Doubt keeps us from abandoning our principles in the name of a passion. Sometimes we want so much to believe that, at any moment, we might embrace a belief too tightly: we are always in danger of our own fundamentalism. But doubt interrogates belief, destabilizes it; doubt keeps us from believing in nonsense. And in seeing the fallibility of the human mind and heart, I find it provides a kind of humility.

In my weaker moments, there is nothing I would rather do than grab the despoilers of our environment, our greedy corporate and political leaders entwined in illusion and selfishness, and throttle them until they admit their pain, see the light, and, in general, agree with my way of seeing things, which must, after all, be right. Hopefully, later I find myself questioning my own beliefs, and I am more patient with those who, like me, are trying to figure things out.

John Locke wrote that we should be very cautious to only act on beliefs of which we are certain, particularly when the liberty of others may be at risk. And since we can never truly be certain about our religious beliefs, we can never coerce them or make them a cause for battle. That would be worth the price of ambivalence.

Doubt is also a vacation from certainty. Not being right is a kind of liberation, a setting down of the burden. Humility is relaxing. In fact, one of the best spiritual teachings I ever heard was simply "Don't Know."

Simplicity of Heart

Says the psalmist: *l'yishrei lev simcha*—to the straight of heart, there is joy. It is not possible to contort the heart into the shape of desire; or to heal on schedule, or to feel on cue. I have felt pseudo-equanimity, pseudo-wisdom, even pseudo-effortlessness. *I am really not trying now. Okay, I guess I am trying too hard to not try. But now I won't try. Wait.*

There is no way out of this twisted logic except to let it drop, and allow the *lev yashar*, the straightforward, simple heart, to simply relax. This cannot be faked.

One of my teachers said, "stopping the war has no limits." You just have to keep giving up, and giving up, and giving up. The simplicity of heart is thus a kind of newness.

Although I have often experienced it as such, loneliness is not, itself, a time of alienation. I have found it to be a portal to a deep and abiding love that exists alongside pain. Yet there is such a fine distinction between falling into the stories of loneliness, which cause a cycle of suffering in the ego, and releasing into the pure feeling of it. It is possible to lose one's way without even noticing it.

To yearn for love is a fundamental human (possibly animal) desire. The aching, too, is to be loved; the pained, intense, entirely justifiable and natural loneliness that we may feel when, like millions of other men and women at this very moment, we are alone.

When I was single, I worried, "If I accept that I am alone, will I never meet my *bashert,* my soul-mate?" If I inhabit my sadness instead of banish it, will I live in gloom?

What I found was that setting down that burden made me more relaxed and thus more confident. I also found that I became more open, more vulnerable, and thus more available for partnership. Sometimes I wonder if my partner would even have liked the old me, trying so hard to be more whole than he was.

Sadness connects us. In the hit film *Inside Out*, which personifies different emotions as characters in the mind of the film's protagonist, it is sadness which brings about her most precious moments with others. Ironically, accepting loneliness becomes a gateway to connection.

I've noticed this doesn't play well at the office, or in politics, or in the media. Those of us in professional roles are meant to be credible, and that means stable, like rocks. We're meant to all be hunky-dory, up for whatever, competent, self-assured. In my experience, this leads to a kind of professional loneliness. When I'm on the receiving end of someone else's facade of competence, I feel alienated and repelled. I wonder what a different model of leadership would look like, one that leads from vulnerability rather than illusion.

This wouldn't mean moping or over-sharing, or picking at the boundaries that make for co-existence in the workplace. For me, it would be the opposite. Residing within loneliness is spacious and secure. It is to see life as it is. It is calm and honest. And when the loneliness of people is visible, I love being with them.

On the Solace of Objects

Bare attention can yield a compensation for the quietude of loneliness. Once boredom is no longer resisted, there is providence all around: the technology created to help bring ease, the living beings upon which we inter-depend. Suppose the attention rests on one material object in the immediate vicinity: a telephone, light switch, whatever. Without the instrumentalizing gaze, the shapes of objects take on their own characters. Allow the quiet; see how the object fulfills its function; imagine the networks of workers, designers, truck drivers who brought it to its location, each serving their own needs but also, in a way, wishing well to you.

From the surrender of agenda comes insights, companionship, even moral imperatives. Resting the attention on appliances is not the way to become the next powerful leader or enviable executive. It is part of a quieter family of joy. It's nothing special. You don't need a degree or a *satori* certificate.

Sadness does not disappear. But with a gentle slowing down and resting of attention, it yields a kind of solace. Now you can hold it, instead of it holding you. It is never a waste of time to pay attention to what normally escapes notice.

And then what happened?

About ten years ago, I was on a meditation retreat and another yogi, a young man in his early twenties, and like many young men, an ardent meditator—told this story.

The yogi was having trouble sleeping, and so, around 1 or 2 in the morning, he crept off to the meditation hall. It was empty, which he expected, and he sat down in his usual place. A few minutes in, a terrible fear came over him. Like a good meditator, he just sat there—but the fear kept coming. Sometimes, there were stories attached: a burglar, even a ghost. He wondered if his family back home was okay, and worried that something had happened. Other times, it was just a pure, unadulterated dread. Something was wrong, somehow. Retelling the story to our teachers, he said it was like being attacked. What should he do with fear like this?

Joseph Goldstein, the well-known American Buddhist teacher, was the first to reply. "And then what happened?" he asked.

The yogi described how he "took the fear as object," watching it, seeing how it felt in the body. Watching it only made it worse; his heartbeat had increased, he noticed, and he was having cold sweats.

"And then what happened?" Joseph asked again. The yogi told of yet another harrowing experience. "And then what happened?" Joseph asked.

The yogi replied, "then my mind began to wander."

Bored at Burning Man

Burning Man is an enormous temporary community that appears in the Nevada desert one week each year. For some people, it's like a festival several miles across, with truly incommunicable expanses of parties, installations, and performances. For others, it's a gathering of some of the most original and creative art (and artists) on the planet. For others still, it is a different way of being in community. There are kids, punks, techies, wanderers, yogis, sculptors, rangers, do-gooders, sparkleponies, grandparents.

It's definitely not just about frolicking in the desert on drugs (which, if you haven't tried it, you should). One of the centers of the city, for example, is a huge temple, built and burned every year, and often a repository for prayers, shrines to departed loved ones, weddings, silence, and tears. It is a place where spoken sadness is beauty. When the temple burned this year, together with a small memorial I made for my mother, I cried, of course.

Amid all of the intensity of living, with life dialed up to 11, and with all that's going on, burning, sparkling, and thumping, it is also possible to have a really lousy time.

I remember one time, several years ago, when I was especially determined to have a Big Experience of some kind on a particular Thursday night. Maybe it would be a huge art project, or I'd meet someone and go adventuring, or have sex, or go dancing in the middle of the desert—something. I was open, I thought.

But it just wasn't happening. I biked, and biked, and biked. I couldn't find any of my friends, didn't click with any strangers, didn't see anything all that new. I actually found myself in the center of Burning Man... bored.

And then miserable.

Finally, *finally*, after what seemed like hours looking for a thrill, or at least a hug—I gave up. Not in a wise, dharmic way; I just stopped trying, after so much failing. I was exhausted.

I thought it would be depressing to give up my quest for awesomeness, but in fact I felt liberated. The burden of my expectation had been dropped, and the sadness that I continued to feel coexisted with a clarity and tranquility that were exquisite. It was easy to say "yes" to what was actually happening, as opposed to what I wanted to happen, and once I did that, I was released.

And because this story takes place at Burning Man, what

happened net was that a giant art car, the size of a tractor-trailer truck but in the form of a huge white whale, pulled up out of nowhere. Which was really pretty awesome.

Queer Gifts

I hid my sexuality, from myself and the world, for over ten years of my adult life. In finally coming to terms with it, and in opening myself to the possibility of love, I thought—well, now I've come out, now all that is behind me.

I was wrong. In fact, I came to see that "coming out of the closet" is not just for queer folks but for everyone. I was astonished at how many closets I was living in, and how many other people seem to have. People closet their spirituality, their joys, their life histories, their talents; they hide loves, transgressions, virtues, and tribes; they bury their essential selves, as if burying something is the best way to preserve it.

And of course, their sadness. There is shame around sadness, as if it's a sign of failure—like you're not doing it right. Even though so many contemplative and philosophical traditions say that sadness is a sign that you *are* doing it right.

The closet does serve its function. Sometimes it is a feature of simple politeness; few people really want an answer to the question, "How are you doing?" And that's fine. Boundaries between public and private enable us to all get along; if we all had to be

The Gate of Tears

perfectly honest with one another all the time, it would be hard for anything to get done.

But many times, it becomes a tomb. I think again about the loneliness in Langston Hughes' "Luck," a poem I return to again and again. The poet has the sense that he is "only" given a glimpse of heaven, rather than love; that this taste is only a crumb fallen from the table of joy. I think this beautiful loneliness derives in large part from his sexuality, and from the double oppressions of race and sexual orientation. It is not that loneliness is the special property of gay people or closeted people—that is why "Luck" can resonate with everyone—but there are particular experiences of it.

As in "Luck," there is a beautiful poetry to this loneliness. It is exquisite, our failure to "only connect," as E.M. Forster's work itself brings to life. Yet having spent several years inhabiting it, I'm happy to have traded poetry for love. The verses of the closet have a poignancy to them; unrequited love is poetically sad. But I'm glad to be done with them.

Another thing I've learned from my experience as a queer man in America is how the cultural understanding of sadness is gendered, and conditioned by misogyny. Most kinds of sadness are marginalized, and seen as forms of weakness, as 'effeminate.'

Ironically, the heteronormative ideal of the hero who is 'never satisfied' and driven to succeed—that, itself, is a recipe for sadness. Yet this work ethic generates cover stories for glossy magazines. The ethic of giving up, meanwhile, does not sell well at all. Sometimes I wonder if the devotees of surrender are, in fact, more numerous than those of struggle, but because they produce less, and consume less, they disappear from history. Thoreau is an exception.

This is part of how I understand Julia/Jack Halberstam's conception of the "Queer Art of Failure." By refusing to engage in these narratives of productivity and generativity—that is, by failing—there is a concomitant refusal to participate in the gendered structures of oppression that prop them up. I will not be a real man, or a lady, or a gentleman; I will gracelessly fail at all of these. I will not be a good consumer or producer; I will not succeed at roles which ought not be succeeded at; I will not conform emotion to parameters of sentiment.

And more, from my own time and place. I will also not be the "leader" I was trained to be, at elite schools and tedious seminars. I will not be anyone's guru. I am a professional, and I have my talents, but I am second tier, too spread out, too uneven. I admit, even to give failure a voice is exhilarating.

Real men don't give up, but I do. I'm quite tenacious in my professional and personal pursuits, but I'm old enough not to believe that talent and tenacity are sufficient. Other people have more. And some people are lucky. To me, this doesn't feel like pessimism; it feels like integrity.

As with the loneliness of Hughes and Forster, it is not that these queer gifts are exclusively the provenance of LGBT people. On the contrary, their value is that they extend beyond us. Perhaps paradoxically, the specificity of identity often enables a greater relatability than a pretense of universalism. There is no universal narrative in any case, and so the first person singular is often more useful (and less patronizing) than the plural. The tears were mine, the gifts are ours.

One should note that Joseph often cried. In fact, there are no less than eight references in the Torah to him doing so. One who has suffered greatly in bad times will cry easily even in good times. His brothers, on the other hand, who had not suffered in their lives, did not even cry when the situation demanded that they should. And as Joseph even cried at the distress of others, he was worthy of attaining his high rank.

Rabbi Zalman Sorotzkin

Most of the paths through the gate of tears lead to a place of internal sufficiency, a profound sense of arrival—a settling-back of the mind that is otherwise often in poses of attraction or repulsion. This is the momentum of freedom.

I am convinced, based on my experiences and those of my students, that this kind of transformation also ripples outward— that it slowly (perhaps too slowly) creates environments of peace, even amid turmoil. As I have written in other books, it's easy to dismiss the current trend of "McMindfulness" and meditation being taught to bankers and businessmen. But I remain of the view that if all of us, bankers included, were able to find the true ground of happiness within, rather than feel compelled to chase after it outside of ourselves, the world would gradually be transformed. And, let's recall, meditation has also transformed the lives of inner-city schoolchildren, battle-scarred veterans, patients in hospitals.

Contemplative quietism naturally leads to interpersonal activism, because the imperative to alleviate suffering arises naturally from a spacious mind and spacious heart. Compassion arises when the obstructions to it are taken away.

There is a further intersection of spirituality and social justice, inner peace and outer. Opening to experiences or memories that are painful tends to open the heart to the pain of others. I recall my feelings of exclusion as an adolescent, and I resolve to fight stigma where I find it today. I recall my immigrant family's economic insecurity, and I resolve to fight for justice for immigrant, disadvantaged, and marginalized families today.

It's easy to mock the "bleeding heart liberal" and think of tree-hugging clichés. But I would take a congressional district full of bleeding-hearts over one cold-hearted conservative who dismisses economic injustice or says that's just how it is. So much of the pose of the well-adjusted is the sequestering and suppression of vulnerability. And it carries with it a patriarchal politics of uncaring—the gendering of 'sentiment' as 'effeminate' and its banishment from 'serious' conversation, as if such conversation is not already conditioned by harsher faculties of the human mind.

In the Biblical story of Joseph, read here by a lesser-known Hasidic master, Rabbi Zalman Sorotzkin, it is precisely Joseph's experiences of hardship—betrayal, inadequacy, violence—that enable him to be a man, which here means not the toughness of masculinist cliché but the very opposite: openness to tears. Joseph's tears are not weakness, but strength. He is emotionally awake, able to experience profound joy. And, in the Biblical tale at least, he is able to effectively lead one of the greatest civilizations of his day. Imagine if our country valued the tears of its leaders as much as their steely resolve and gritty determination.

Sherri Mandell, whose son was killed in a terrorist attack, writes of her simultaneous alienation and solidarity with those in her community:

> And now I am the woman whom people don't know how to address. I fill people with the dread of death. I remind them that death is around us. But by being the person nobody wants to be, I can console others because I am not separate from anybody's pain. I can't distance myself. I don't have that luxury. I can be there for others because my suffering includes so many of the permutations of pain.

I hear an echo of the Joseph story here. Mandell's wound is open; everyone knows who she is, and the enormity of her loss makes them uncomfortable. Yet precisely in that open, naked, unhideable woundedness, she is connected to the pain of others. Her empathy is hard-won, and unasked-for. But imagine her learned capacity to bear that pain, to hold it, to act on the basis of its reality. She embodies this capacity, has no choice but to do so; her tears are strength.

The contrary Biblical ideal of Joseph's empathy is echoed in Exodus' commandment not to oppress strangers, since "you know the heart of a stranger." From the knowledge of the marginalized comes an empathy for the marginalized. From its suppression comes only inhumanity.

The Dream of the Magician

You've got to go out on a limb sometimes because that's
where the fruit is.

Will Rogers

In high school, all I wanted, but didn't even know that I
wanted, was a magician to suddenly appear in my life and peel
back the grey curtain of my existence to reveal a magical, rain-
bow world underneath.

Now in middle age, I know that world exists—multiple ones,
in fact—places of discovery, awakening, ecstasy, consciousness,
creativity, connection, love, all totally unknown to me when I
was younger. But it took me years to find them, especially in that
pre-Internet age. There were a few hints in my twenties: a couple
of peak experiences, usually with the help of one substance or
other; some spiritual highs in my Orthodox Jewish years; and,
as the shells began to break, some wonderful times with music
and friends and lovers. Really, though, the transformation didn't
begin until 2001, when at age thirty, my old life shattered and
I felt I had nothing to lose by jumping off the cliff, and either
falling or flying or both.

One early sign: I saw *Dead Poets Society* at age 17, and was
instantly convinced to seize the day, gather rosebuds while I
may, and, along the way, bond with other thirsty, intellectual-
ly-minded young men. When I put Mr. Keating's advice into
practice, though, I made two mistakes. First, I mistook the form
for the freedom, thinking that poetry specifically was the point.
I thus wrote a lot of poetry—much of which, ironically, led to

a cul-de-sac of early-'90s irony and cynicism. Second, I did not understand how much I had fallen in love (or lust) with the movie's tragic hero, Neil Perry.

There was no Mr. Keating in my teenage life: no teacher, no older peer, not even a friend. I suppose if there had been, I might've prospered sooner. As it was, I did my best. I got into the Beat poets, and the Beatles, but where anything was happening contemporaneously, I had no idea. It all seemed miles away, growing up in the suburbs, in Florida. So I appreciated the 1960s, which in this youthful metonymy stood for creativity, free expression, and living life fully—as opposed to the 1980s, which to me stood for superficiality, football games, and conformity. I had neither the aptitude nor the interest in what my peers seemed to be doing. I was a gay kid closeted from himself, so I had no idea what I was supposed to do with girls. And I was at the bottom of the social food chain. I imitated as best I could. But I spent such large chunks of my adolescence editing a computer club newsletter, playing computer games, and being by myself. I was alone, and isolated. I had no idea how to make my life extraordinary.

From this vantage point, there's a sort of sadness, or at least a wistfulness, looking back on those times. They do seem to be times lost. I know that the experiences of those years shaped me into the person I am now, for better as well as for worse, and so I try not to regret. I am aware of how privileged and fortunate I was, with two loving parents and an upper-middle-class economic existence. I am mindful, too, of a quip, from one Lord Clark, to the effect of, "All intellectuals complain about their school days. This is ridiculous."

But mostly, I admit, there is regret. Imagine, if there had just been one person: a boy, maybe, or a teacher, or *someone* to rip open that junior-high school facade, and tell me the secret that there are whole other worlds out there, don't waste your time with these people, come with me, and I'll show you a life so intense, so *alive*, that they can't even dream of it.

Later, I would play the Mr. Keating role myself. At the summer camp where I worked in my late teens and twenties, I turned the ultimate frisbee team into my own Dead Poets Society, complete with scorn for the normals, counterculture values, and even some actual poetry. And as a Hebrew High School teacher in my twenties, I tried to influence my kids to... what? To seize the day, I suppose. To see things differently. To make fun of the mainstream. Simple stuff. *Catcher in the Rye* stuff. But stuff that no one had told me five or ten years earlier.

But was I seizing the day myself? At the time, I was in law school, albeit for partly noble reasons. I was deep in the closet, hopelessly and sometimes pathetically in love with straight boys. And while I was going out and drinking and seeing some shows, none of those things, when I look back on them now, seem that extraordinary. All along, I was being creative: writing, painting, eventually writing music once I taught myself guitar. Yet none of those had much of an outlet. One photography show at Yale, and a few poems in literary magazines. Otherwise, I treated my creativity as a hobby.

In 2001, my girlfriend and I were riding in a cab when our taxi was struck by a tow truck. She broke two legs, and I suffered a serious concussion that permanently affected my short-term memory. Within six months, we had broken up—maybe I wasn't bisexual after all—and Burning Man showed me that I could have those wonderful, intimate conversations that previously I'd only read about in books. Eventually, meditation and spiritual practice cracked open my soul to possibilities of love I'd never even known about. It has been a long journey, and it continues.

I realize that the dream of the magician is, in some ways, an adolescent dream. There's a reason *Dead Poets Society* was set in a high school; just "going for it" in some vague sense is, well, a kind of high school/college thing to do.

But I think it's still a good dream to nourish. It's interesting to me to see some of my peers all grown up, yet never having taken those early, naïve steps on a spiritual, artistic, philosophical, or just plain hedonistic seizing-the-day journey. I'm sure their lives are fulfilling, with kids and family and the rest. But to never have escaped the box you were born into! The dream has political import, too: part of seeing the box is to see how it entails oppression.

There are many alchemies that spring from those years of frustration and pain, some productive, others less so. With the approach I've described in this book, I have learned not to dwell on regret, and also not to push it away. Perhaps most importantly, I know and love people who are growing and flourishing, and who inspire me. At best, it is a symbiotic relationship, mutually opening, daring, provoking, laughing, and inspiring. We are each other's magicians, performing at a kind of carnival, in which I get to grow wiser and kinder, and experience more ecstasy than I'd ever thought possible.

Sometimes I wonder if the admission ticket could have been bought with a bit less pain. I suspect it could not have been.

Shakey: An Essay on Anger

I called him Shakey, because he couldn't sit still. About forty-five or fifty years old, with thick white hair up front and a bald spot on the crown of his head, Shakey sat near me during a forty-day meditation retreat I went on several years ago. He moved constantly: during a 45 minute sit, he almost never was still for more than one minute at a time. (Yes, I timed it once, using my breaths as measurements—he never made it past eight breaths without moving.) Shifting his posture, moving his feet, scratching—and always making noise.

For forty days.

Now, in the context of insight meditation practice, a disturbing noise is not, itself, wrong. It breaks your concentration a bit, but in terms of mindfulness, it just becomes your focus for a moment. You might make a small mental note of the hearing of it ("hearing") and then, perhaps, any emotional response that arises (anger, amusement, whatever). If the attention wanes, you return to the breath; if not, you note something else. The point is, it doesn't really matter what the object of your attention is; what matters is how you relate to it, whether you're letting it come and go, or whether you're grabbing onto it or pushing it away.

In theory, then, Shakey was not a disturbance. He was just the predominant object. The very predominant object.

In practice, though, it wasn't working out. I was getting lost in anger, unable to build concentration. I spun out long, long stories about maybe Shakey was disabled somehow, or had ADD.

(Shakey, by the way, is Neil Young's longtime nickname. Apologies to Neil.) Or, who knows, maybe he was just totally clueless, or maybe there could be some way, somehow, that I could talk to the teachers....

I got lost in anger, and lost in thought.

Of course, anger, too, can be just another object of attention, just like the sounds Shakey was making. It arises, it passes. It causes suffering. It's not really me. All the key points are right there. And it can be experienced, like sadness or anything else, as a present-moment, embodied experience. For example, I learned, by observation, that I experience anger mostly in my arms—a heat, or a quaking—together with constriction of the jaw, tension in the mind, and an increased heart rate. This in contrast to how I often respond to anger, which is to figure out what it is I'm angry about, and how right I must be.

Well, that all sounds rosy, but it often doesn't work, and it didn't work with my stuff about Shakey. For me, anger is not merely another object of attention; it swallows me up. In fact, of all the emotional demons I've wrestled, anger has been the hardest for me to coexist with. When I get angry, it often gets me. With Shakey, I could not resist going into the story: what was so wrong with him, and why I was either right or wrong to respond the way I did. Maybe I am really being too judgmental. Maybe I'm a lazy practitioner. Maybe my concentration is too weak. Maybe the teachers should let this guy know that he's disturbing other people.

Sigh.

My anger at Shakey actually had little to do with the physical sounds that he was making. One morning, a truck (propane? gas?) parked itself right outside the meditation hall and made a truly irritating noise, whining and varying its pitch, for about half an hour. No problem. The truck was just doing what it had to do, the motors were running the way they were supposed to, and, while perhaps an unfortunate bit of timing, it was really no big deal. It was actually kind of funny—here were a hundred people, coming from all over the world for some silence, and then a truck parks right next to them and whines. Loudly.

In contrast to the truck, I imagined that Shakey had moral responsibility; he should know better. Worse, while the truck was a temporary problem, Shakey was long-term. And I was powerless to do anything about it. I couldn't tell him to stop moving. I couldn't really complain to the teachers—they'd probably just tell me to watch my mind and note my anger. I just had to sit there.

I tried to see that anger was present because I was hurting. I wanted to be able to sit undisturbed, and I couldn't. So I tried some compassion for myself, too. But that didn't really stick either.

To be fair to myself here, I wasn't always angry at Shakey. Sometimes the noise didn't bother me at all. Sometimes I had a lot of compassion for him, because if you keep moving around like that, you never gain the stillness of body and mind that's so valuable and so rare. I was sincerely sad on Shakey's behalf sometimes. For a while, anyway.

What finally cracked it, for me, was the experience of nonself. I had learned intellectually, years ago, that the conventional modern subject—the self—is only a way of looking at learned behaviors, conditioned by hundreds or thousands of other phenomena (including genetics). You learned these words, learned how to think them, learned how to feel about them, learned opinions by which you judge them. It's all just cause and effect—not self.

But map is not territory—and now I saw what before I had only heard. All that was happening was a great series of empty, conditioned phenomena—God, in other words—including Shakey moving, including the truck, including every sound and vision. And what arises inside the mind is part of the circuit too. When the conditions for anger are present, anger arises, just like an itch, or just like the sound that will arise when Shakey's feet scrape the floor. The feet shift; the sound is made; the response arises.

This was a sweet surrender. The conditions were present, the phenomena arose. And the play of life goes on, as Leonard Nimoy used to say. What's the point of being angry with anger? And without the itch of anger, there was less of a desire to act on it. Okay... anger... it feels like this. It's like that.

Even the Dalai Lama gets angry sometimes, according to statements he's made. Being awake does not mean that the infinite chains of causality will be broken. Cause, effect; stimulus, response. All part of the plan. A feature, not a bug.

My father used to have a bad temper; like many men of his generation, he would yell in restaurants, and get upset at politicians, football games, and pool-cleaning equipment. I rarely saw him get violent, but I was still terrified by him when I was younger and embarrassed by him when I was a little older. I see him in myself when I get angry for forgetting my cell phone somewhere, or furious at hitting my head—and I don't like to see that part of him in me. I feel unworthy, and I feel like a fraud, as if all my meditation practice and teaching is bullshit.

So I surrender even to the inability to surrender; even to the times when anger wins. God is Shakey, God is the sound he makes, God is the arising of anger, the feeling of it, the judging it, the letting go of it. There's no getting away from the endless series of empty phenomena rolling on. It's always now and always here and nothing else remains. It is also, thank God, the passing away.

In that "thank God," I think, is the beautiful conundrum of religion.

part three:
merging

There is nothing so whole as a broken heart.
-Rabbi Menachem Mendel of Kotsk

The Gate of Tears

Not Saying No

The Vietnamese Buddhist teacher Thich Nhat Hanh has written that there is cloud in every piece of paper, because without the cloud there would be no rain to grow the trees that produced the paper. Likewise, the paper is made up of the logger, the mill, the sun—in fact there is nothing in the paper that is not dependent upon something else. Nor will the paper exist forever; eventually it will return to its true reality, which is non-existence. And this is true, of course, for all of the elements that made up the paper; it is not that the cloud, sun, or logger is more real.

So what *is* the paper? From a non-theistic perspective, it is an empty phenomenon, rolling on. From a theistic perspective, it is a temporary ripple on the ocean of God. Same reality, described in different terms, with different associations and moods. The central point is that it's not a piece of paper—not ultimately.

The mind is not quite like a piece of paper; it has evolved to be very active. It is a tool that ensures the propagation and blossoming of the species, and we use it so often and so seamlessly that most of us actually identify ourselves with our minds (and hearts, but I'm taking the two together here.) The mind thinks temporally, dualistically, conceptually, and allows us to do amazing things.

It is also desiring. With close, contemplative attention, one can notice that the mind either wants or doesn't want almost everything it encounters. Objects in a room, people we meet—

we immediately and without noticing attach an attractive or aversive label (or both) to them. Some things we just mildly want—ice cream. Others we want a great deal—food when we are hungry, toys and technology. And others we want so much that we suffer intensely when they are denied us.

Somtimes it's possible to perceive directly how these desires arise, without any need for "me" to do anything about them. Over time, the mind does start to resemble a piece of paper, made up entirely of other things, not separate from those things.

What is left over? In the theistic perspective, God is simply whatever is left over when the self is taken away. This "God" is always present, regardless of the feelings in the heart or notions in the mind. Sadness, sorrow, heartbreak, and pain still appear, just as they always do. So does bliss. These are all different masks of the One.

In this way of speaking, sadness is God in a minor key. It's not just okay to feel sad—it is holy to feel sad, if that is what is happening now. When I push away sadness and try only to think happy thoughts, I am denying "What Is"—denying God. It's as if everything is holy—except this.

The gate of tears is a sustained and gentle Yes—or at least, a not saying No; not capitulating to this quite natural tendency of the mind, to mistake what is in front of us for something other than God.

The Gods of Drowning

I've tried to convey, in these pages, the practices of "being with" whatever arises in the body, mind, and heart (Part One), and some of the redemptive aspects of the shadow sides of that experience (Part Two). Both aspects of the gate of tears resist the therapeutic momentum to change these ways of being in order to help us be more adaptive and happy, and the instinctual one to hold onto the good stuff and push away the rest.

In this third part of the book, I will talk about how this surrender, this willingness to be thoroughly subsumed by sadness and dissolved into it, is a religious path as well.

Thanks to evolution, happiness is unnatural. If we were all perfectly happy with what we already have, we wouldn't strive for more. We wouldn't reproduce, wouldn't compete for scarce resources—and we'd be selected right out of the species. So it's human nature to be unhappy, and to work to address that unhappiness by taking action, building things, having children, nurturing them, and building cooperative communities of love. All these things feel right because we've been born and bred to do them. And that is fine.

But there are contrary momentums as well: toward resting, settling back, savoring. These, too, are natural, in their way.

I used to experience this contrariness as being like someone nearly drowning in water or mud, but managing to be with it, to stay alive and breathe. Instinct would tell me to fight the drowning and clamber out somehow, but I would train myself just to stay afloat in the muck. In some ways, this way of seeing the contemplative path was inspiring, since it emboldened me to be some kind of Dharma warrior, sitting there on the cushion for hours. But mostly, it was an unhelpful way of seeing. The whole image contains an inevitable aura of resistance—of fighting, enduring, persisting. It was like that joke about how many Jewish mothers it takes to change a lightbulb. "None, dahling, I'll just sit in the dark."

Over the years, in the wake of loss, breakup, loneliness, heartbreak, and occasional rebirth, my heart has learned a different relationship to drowning. At times, there was so much pain that I couldn't fight it if I tried. And I did try. But if I had really been standing in a deep pile of mud, it would've covered me long ago. And so I learned to let it happen. Not fighting, not even floating, but drowning. Fortunately, I found I can breathe underwater. Instead of fighting to stay afloat in the humiliation, anger, sadness; in the midst of the muck of pain, it is possible to sink down, and down, and down… and sometimes, it all disappears, like an illusion, a construct of the mind. I thought I needed air, but I don't. I can breathe in the mud, and the act of surrendering to it brings relaxation and release.

At such times, the yielding seems like an embrace of the non-dual, the God that is *yotzer or u'vorei choshech*, Former of light and Creator of darkness. This God offers a different kind of comfort from traditional religion; not the love of the Friend, or the assurance of a father figure, but the sense of being surrounded and filled by What Is. This God is not necessarily nice or just; it's the God of cancer wards as well as summer pastures, of war as well as love. This is the God that asks us if we can handle the truth: that both evil and good are holy.

But there is another God of Drowning, too: the personal God, the emotional one, the one to whom I cry. I cannot say whether I "believe" in such a God; belief seems like the wrong faculty of mind. The personal is the devotional, the place of faith and trust: *hinei el yeshuati, evtach v'lo efchad.* Behold, God is my salvation; I will trust and not fear. When it is hard to allow the drowning, I still call for help. Of course, this personal, devotional, anthropomorphic God is largely projection; it's a way of seeing more than a thing that is seen. But as projection, God is a precious Friend, a beloved, a companion. Is not love, too, such a myth?

My religious life oscillates between these poles, these two Gods of Drowning. At times, I love to think of God in what are essentially human terms. This is the God to whom I pray—and of whom I say "whom." This is the God that is You. Other times, I love the clarity of the more atheistic, nondual God: What Is, YHVH. The great silence that is the impersonal universe of empty phenomena rolling on, with no one directing the traffic. Sometimes I want a hand to rescue me from the drowning, and other times I just want to drown, to merge, to dissolve into You.

I have already admitted that this path is neither for everyone nor the dominant path among religious traditions. It goes better with silent retreats than with raucous parties. But its truthfulness, for me, is more comfortable than any comfort. For me, truth is more relaxing than myth.

Not wallowing in the mud, not turning it over, not explaining, not repelling; total surrender, total release. But letting go, letting drown, letting expand, letting relax. Breathing while drowning, the attention naturally comes to the present, with nothing pulling it elsewhere. And then, with a breath, without hope, expectation, or object, a simple wish of love.

All of It

The Jewish morning prayer service begins, significantly, with the words of a non-Jewish prophet, Balaam, who had been sent to curse the Israelites by a foreign king. The Torah tells that on his journey to curse Israel, Balaam had been blind to the reality of God's presence. Even his donkey had seen that angels were accompanying them (and blocking their way), but Balaam was on an errand. Maybe you know this feeling, when you're so busy rushing and worrying and planning that you do not see what is around you. I certainly do.

After a series of extraordinary events, Balaam does finally open his eyes, and by the time he arrives at the Israelite camp, he is filled with insight. Instead of a curse, he says: *mah tovu ohalecha ya'akov, mishkenotecha yisrael.* Which means: how good are your tents, Jacob; your dwelling places, Israel.

The sentence is a parallel construction of two clauses: one about the tents of Jacob, the other about the dwelling places of Israel. Symbolically, these are two aspects of human life. Jacob's first act was to grasp the ankle of his twin brother, Esau, as they came out of the womb. As a boy, he lived in the shadow of his older, stronger brother, and he schemed to obtain Esau's blessing and birthright. Jacob is the grasper, the small-mind, the part that hurts and yearns and cheats and steals—all of that shadow. He lives in a closed tent.

But after his transformation, after he wrestles the angel and is renamed Israel, he lives in "dwelling places of Israel." Not only has his name changed, but his dwelling, too: the Hebrew word mishkan is also the word for the Divine sanctuary. And of course, his transformation is appealing. Don't we all want that—to be God-wrestlers, or abiding in expanded states of mind? The point is to be more like Israel and less like Jacob—right?

Not quite.

Balaam does not say that only Israel's dwelling places are good. Nor does he say how great it is when our finite tents are transformed into places for the Infinite. Rather, both sides are *tov*, good. We are here, with bodies, with hearts, minds, and souls. We cry when we are hurt and laugh when we are joyful. This is *tov*—good. It is *tov* when we make our lives into dwelling places for holiness, and it is also *tov* when we are suffering.

And not merely good. According to the Zohar, the masterwork of the Kabbalah, the word *Mah*, which ordinarily means 'what' or 'how,' is a signifier of the *Shechinah*, the Divine Presence Herself. So when Balaam says *mah tovu*, he isn't just saying how good are your tents; he is saying how God are your tents.

Goodness, wholeness, okay-ness, the Presence of God, however you understand what it is you most want to be—it is present both at expanded and inspired moments of 'Israel,' and times of challenging, contracted 'Jacob.' In this way of seeing, God is not a man in the sky, or a particularly good spiritual feeling, or even a moral law, but everywhere and in all of creation, right here, now, in your mind and outside your mind, with no inside or outside. I've described this in other books; the point here is that Jacob is also Israel; samsara is nirvana; the contracted heart is of the same nature as the open one.

"This Is It"—this moment of experience, even if it has taken the color of sadness, is the Big It, God, Enlightenment, the Now, Being, What Is. Balaam's blessing suggests as much, and it's possible to feel it to be so. There is no outside to the One Being around you and inside you. Through the gate of tears, all of our experience is holy, even those parts which our egos regret or despise.

Don't try to "get it" if you're not getting it. Surrender into not getting it, and you've got it.

When I Speak of Sadness, I Seek the Symbols of God

When we speak of serious matters, not necessarily in a dour or humorless tone, but with a sincerity of purpose; when silence overwhelms the trivialities of the everyday; and when our attitudes and dispositions melt before an awe greater than our condescensions—it is at these times when the vocabulary of religion takes on, for some of us, its true character.

Applied to science or politics, religion is a poor substitute for reason. Its myths, never meant to be empirical, harden into nonsensical dogmas and irrational beliefs, whose preposterousness requires a fundamentalist certitude on behalf of the credulous. When they are married to the violence of politics, they ossify into rigid codes and morals.

But when the heart is cracked open, the insensible becomes relatable. "Only the nonsensical is at ease with the Absolute," wrote the poet James Broughton. And for all the exasperation of being lumped together with the pious and the ignorant, it would be dishonest to pretend as if I have outgrown the vocabulary and symbols of Judaism, shopworn and abused, outmoded and nonsensical—yet perhaps for that reason resonant in a way that more recent and more sophisticated ideologies are not. When my heart speaks, it speaks in this language.

This kind of religion is not a matter of opinion, belief, tribe, identity, salvation, creation, or hunch that there is a cosmic Santa meting out justice in some secret, special way. It is a matter of love; of an interpersonal vocabulary of meaning; of imagination and the marking of time.

Of course, for many, being religious is absolutely about opinions—about God, Bible, Tribe. It may mean following rules, and even believing those rules to be absolutely true.

But none of this really matters to me. I have more in common with an atheist who dances than with supposedly pious men who are asleep in their lives. The religion in which I am interested is about being in love with the world, and, yes, sucking the marrow out of life, in whatever mode suits our temperament. I don't care about the God you don't believe in; I care that there is a source for inspiration. Here is Schleiermacher, the consummate German Romantic, writing in 1799:

> The universe exists in uninterrupted activity and reveals itself to us every moment. Every form that it brings forth, every being to which it gives a separate existence according to the fullness of life, every occurrence that spills forth from its rich, ever-fruitful womb, is an action of the same upon us. Thus to accept everything individual as part of

a whole and everything limited as a representation of infinite, is religion.

On Religion: Speeches to its Cultured Despisers, p. 105

For Schleiermacher, religion is about cultivating and expressing our intuition of the infinite. And so, he knew, those "cultured despisers" of churches, hierarchies, and dogmas are often more religious than those who uphold them. Precisely because of their true religiosity, they critique the structures that some people have chosen to build around religion: myths, churches, hierarchies. There can be no authentic system of religion, Schleiermacher wrote, any more than there could be a system of intuition. If what we mean, when we talk about "God" is not a person, not a consciousness, not a spirit, but simply, What Is, then the question is not one of existence or faith but of symbol. Does the world merit being named God, or not?

Sometimes this language helps, and sometimes it does not. But when I speak of sadness, I seek the symbols of God, the sequences of myth, and the patterns of old religion. It is not that I suspend disbelief; I find the question of belief irrelevant. Now, is this "religion" according to everyone? No. I am aware of that every time I step foot in a synagogue to say *kaddish* for my mother. But I am there, aren't I? Precisely when I am at my most desperate—that is, my most open—the personal God reappears, as if She or He has been playfully hiding in plain view all along. Somehow the doubt seems beside the point; not wrong, but the correct answer to a different question. And so I contradict myself, I deny my reason. Indeed, "there are no atheists in foxholes." At least not this one.

The Gate of Tears

We are without control over our lives, and there is only mystery. We have no idea. In the face of this realization, tears lie deeper than reason.

Sick Enough

"Most people are not sick enough for religion," the scholar of mysticism Louis Dupré once said. I was in his class on the philosophy of religion, taking a break from (or perhaps fleeing) my law school life in 1996. I think he was paraphrasing Kierkegaard.

At the time—defensive, closeted, Orthodox Jewish, arrogant—I rejected the assertion. I'm not religious because I'm deficient in some way, I thought, or trying to compensate my way back to normalcy. I'm religious because I want to rise above it—to a height of holiness, to the *summum bonum* of human experience: mysticism, union with God.

I'm quite happy to be over that arrogance.

For many people, religion is straightforward: it fulfills social functions, brings us together, marks important moments in life. But what about the "spiritual but not religious," the monastic, the contemplative? Are we exquisitely sensitive, with souls of poets? Or are we, maybe, more needy, more scarred, more... sick? Or, another option, is it simply a matter of taste?

Let's exclude one proposal: the lazy notion that spirituality is an opiate. If this is its role, it is surely a failure. Religion ought to heighten the mystery, not resolve it. At its most poetic, it disquiets as much as it soothes. Likewise, contemporary spirituality; the secularized forms of meditation and yoga may be seen, today, like ways to relax, but if they are taken seriously, they are often not relaxing at all. They reveal truths that are sometimes difficult to see. As Lama Surya Das said, "Truth is about getting free, not getting high."

The formula of "you're not sick enough for religion" implies that it might be better to be healthy. But Dupré is himself a mystic, suggesting that the exchange is worthwhile. Better to be sick and awake, we might say, than healthy and asleep. "To others, only heaven," Hughes writes; it is unclear if "only" is ironic.

Or perhaps, as the earlier epigraph from Rabbi Sorotzkin suggests, tears are not a sign of deficiency but of nobility of character. Joseph has developed empathy; that is why he cries. Not sickness, but a deeper health. You are meant to cry, because life is cruel and death is worse—not *only* to cry, of course, but when it is appropriate to do so, which it often is.

Human beings have a wide range of emotional capacities. To me, it seems sad not to be moved at the sight of a glorious sunset, or concerned about the ecological collapse of the planet, or empathetic enough to try to understand what it might be to be hungry, disadvantaged, stigmatized. It is clear that one may be happy without any of these experiences. But it feels somehow hollow to me.

On an intuitive level, I don't think that religion, art, therapy, and medication are meant to return us to some base level of well-adjusted okayness. Then again, I'm also not sure about Krishnamurti's maxim that "it is no measure of health to be well adjusted to a profoundly sick society." At times, I admit I envy those people who seem to have a perfect fit between what they want and what society has to offer. It must be lovely to have such a congruence between self and world. So I think it's an open question whether the spiritual path is but a consolation, or a well-worthy recompense. I'm not sure I had a choice but to take it.

Faith

Faith, in its purest form, is inchoate. Unlike faith-in-something, which has a cognitive object, it is a disposition of trust, without any object at all. It's an attitude, a way of being, that has no particular object and no theory to which it is beholden. ("Trusting your own deepest experience," Sharon Salzberg calls it in her book *Faith*). It's only when faith is combined with ideas, particularly about how the world should be, or about how it came to be the way it is now, that faith translates into self-deception, or distraction, or even danger.

Faith, unlike theology, is composed of tears, not theorems. I cannot make Jewish theology cohere, despite years of God-wrestling and graduate degrees in the study of it. And even within my Jewish theology, crying out to the nondual is ridiculous. But sometimes I do like to cry. *Ana adonai, hoshi'a na*—please, God, save me. In a small irony, our tears fall all the more readily if we are crying to a God in which we're not sure we believe.

What is the part of the heart that cries anyway?

"There is nothing so whole as a broken heart," the Kotsker rebbe taught, knowing from his own life the taste of melancholy and the way in which the heart's yearning opens us to experience Reality. The Jewish path is one of love and tears and fear and doubt. The broken heart is what I mean by God's heart breaking.

An Expression

The legendary patriarchs of the Jewish religion were all men in great pain.

Abraham, the progenitor of Judaism, Christianity, and Islam, felt himself called to leave his entire world behind, leave the house of his fathers, and settle in a new land he did not know. He was promised that he would be the father of multitudes (as his original name, Avram, implies), yet he was childless into old age, and his beloved wife Sarah did not conceive until they were so elderly and so anguished that she and Abraham laughed at the very idea. Abraham sent his son Ishmael into the wilderness, and nearly sacrificed his son Isaac at the command of God. What unimaginable pain must this man have felt?

Isaac, nearly murdered by his own father, does not speak again until he is near death. He is acted-upon, traumatized, never able to become the master of his own life. A wife is found for him.

She tricks him. His son deceives him. If the pain of Abraham is caused by his actions, the pain of Isaac is caused by his inaction.

And Jacob, the grasper; the mama's boy who was not a man, who stayed at home and cooked while his stronger, macho brother hunted. His queer, cunning, grasping mind devised stratagems to obtain what it wanted—but is he ever happy? He labors for seven years to 'obtain' a wife, is tricked, and labors another seven years. His beloved Rachel dies in childbirth. For twenty years, he believes his beloved son Joseph to be dead. His daughter is raped. Though ostensibly all ends well for Yisrael, the success comes at a cost.

And surely the matriarchs must have suffered more, even though their suffering has been largely muted by patriarchal history. Sarah, in danger of rape in Egypt, pretends to be Avram's sister; she is childless throughout most of her life in a culture that valued children above all; and when she hears that Abraham has gone to sacrifice her son to God, the midrash tells us, she dies with a whispering cry. Rebecca deceives her husband on his deathbed; what does this tell us about their love? Leah, married to a man who openly does not love her as much as he loves her sister; Rachel, who dies so young. And Hagar, Bilhah, and Zilpah, women who, we must assume, are never loved with the whole hearts of their husbands who are also their masters—and who have been virtually silenced by our subsequent tradition.

Judaism is a religion born of great, deep pain. As Tolstoy said, unhappy families are unhappy each in their own way.

The Amidah, a central prayer of the Jewish liturgy, contains the line *eloheinu v'elohei avoteinu, elohei avraham, elohei yitzhak, elohei yaakov.* (Some also add corresponding phrases for the matriarchs as well.) The first half of the line acknowledges the

One as 'Our God and God of our ancestors'—this is the God we inherit in our tradition, probably with many misgivings, and who unites us into a single faith community. But the second half is diversity, not unity; subjectivity, not objectivity. The 'God of our fathers' is not the only God the text contains. The 'God of Abraham' is different from the 'God of Isaac' and different from the 'God of Jacob.' And each reflects a different kind of sadness.

Perhaps religion, in this sense, is less an antithesis to suffering than a poetic expression of its simultaneous unity and diversity.

The Cry of Honesty

Jesus Christ, crucified and near death, asks, "My God, my God, why have you forsaken me?" *Eloi, eloi, lama sabachtani.*

One American Zen master once said to me that this was not really a question, and not really asked. It was a cry, and it was cried out in agony, pain, and despair.

How could the Son of God possibly be in such despair? Throughout the passion, Christ displays equanimity, refusing the pleas of his disciples to run away, refusing to defend himself before his accusers. He is the model of detachment. But he cracks. How is this possible?

Perhaps it is possible both to know that one is not alone, and to feel that one is indeed forsaken. The enlightened Christ does not deny his humanity, or leave it behind like some old garment which is no longer necessary. This body, beautiful and broken; this heart, sad and open; this mind.

So there is an honesty here, an integrity. Christ's pain is transparent; it is not suppressed. It is what is happening: agony, despair. The truthfulness of suffering is preferable to its papering over.

Of course, God does not reply to Christ, in some mystical experience, and does not lift the burden of his suffering. This is not the answer. Presence is the answer. "It is accomplished."

Radical Non-Evil

When the Psalmist sings *Na'ar hayiti, gam zakanti, v'lo raiti tzadik ne'ezav*—I was a youth, and now have grown old, and I have never seen a righteous person abandoned—was the poet naïve? Did he (or she) lead a sheltered life, in which no one suffered? Surely King David, the traditional author of the psalms, saw righteous people of his generation betrayed and even killed. Surely an anonymous poet would have as well.

But suffering is not the same as abandonment. Of course, righteous people suffer, get sick, die, and are the victims of outrageous injustice. But perhaps some of them do not experience abandonment. I am not so righteous, but perhaps someone is.

Some traditional religionists say that it will all work out in the end: sins punished, good deeds rewarded. And perhaps there is even some Divine plan, in which a few eggs must be broken in order to create the omelets of this or that higher good. Such answers are logically sufficient to explain evil away, but their logic only serves to demonstrate how irrelevant that realm is to the question we are really asking. Really, we want to understand not the abstract reality of suffering but the existential presence of it. How can *this* be reconciled, at all, with a benevolent ordering principle of the universe? Not in its abstraction, but in its particularity. *This, this*—this feeling, this absolute refutation of all forms of reasoning, of the very *existence* of explanation. It is this deep, subjective appreciation of evil that makes the neat answers of conventional theology seem like frivolity.

This is also why consolations of greater suffering—that others have it far worse than you or I—are so unlikely to console. They are not false; certainly whatever pain we feel is less objectively intense than that of victims of torture or debilitating disease. But they suggest that the thing to do is deny what is happening because of something else that is happening. The gate of tears asks that we deny nothing at all.

The Book of Job, which addresses itself to questions of suffering, is often misunderstood in this regard. Job is often portrayed as a steadfast, righteous man who does not abandon his belief in God or give himself over to despair. In fact, his grief is so great that his friends do not recognize him when they first approach. Job's first words are not confident, religious ones; he wishes he had never been born. He cries out in pain. His friends try to offer explanations—it must be punishment, God has a plan —but Job disagrees. "How can a man be just with God?" he asks in Chapter 9. There is no explanation.

When God answers Job out of the whirlwind, there is no explanation. God's response is only to deny the validity of the question. "Where were you, when I laid the foundations of the Earth? Does the rain have a father? Who gave birth to the dewdrops?" There is no answer to any of these questions—Job's or God's.

Answers to questions of theodicy replace experience with a story about why the experience is not justified, or is transitory, or is less to be loved than other mind-states. In fact, no suffering is justified, or unjustified; it is not something that is to be described in that way.

This is the deep joy of the contemplative that coexists with sadness, and even with evil. Life is not a happy affair, and not explicable on some deep level. When explanation is no longer sought, by the heart as well as the mind, a part of suffering drops.

It is for this reason that I part company with the best-known author of Jewish books on pain and suffering, Harold Kushner. Kushner, writing after the death of his son, decides that, as between a God who could allow such suffering but chooses not to, and a God who could not have prevented it, he, Kushner, prefers the latter. Kushner's book is far more radical than its bestselling status suggests; it is a rejection of a thousand years of theology. Which is fine, if it brings comfort—first and foremost, to Kushner himself. But I admit to not understanding the world which he seeks to describe. Kushner's God is a non-omnipotent deity, combining powerlessness and anthropomorphism. It is a God of What Ought to Be, which I do not recognize as "God." His deity would help, but cannot. Thus we may retain the aspects of religious rhetoric which posit good and evil, place God wholly on the side of the good, and continue to venerate this God for conforming to our most profound wishes of how the world should be.

I do not reject this world so much as fail to comprehend it. The world I inhabit is one in which bad things happen to good people, not because God is powerless to stop them, but because all kinds of things happen all the time. It does not console me to suppose that there is a fantastic, meaning-making deity out there who, unfortunately, was not able to spare a righteous person from death. I have not experienced what Kushner has experienced. But to sit squarely opposite the facts of the human condition, to recognize their inexplicability, and to hold, without believing, the fervent desire for life to be otherwise—this, to me, is a better response to evil than fantasy. There are tales of divine potency in every religious tradition, but reason, fact, truth—these I find more comforting than even the most appealing of stories. An answer that saves a cherished myth is, to me, less comforting than the lack of any answer whatsoever.

Sadness in Mystical Perspective

Who experiences sadness?

In a mystical perspective, there are two aspects to that which is experienced—ecstasy, sadness, anger, joy—which certain Hasidic traditions express as *yesh*, something, and *ayin*, nothing. As in Zen (and much of Mahayana Buddhism), it is not either/or, but both/and. On the one hand, all of these perceptions certainly exist from what the forgotten Hasidic master Rabbi Aaron of Staroselse calls "our point of view." They are experienced in the soul, mind, heart, and body, and are as real as anything we know. Our perspective is defined by a thousand cultural constructions, genetic accidents, and history. This perspective sees the world as *yesh*, as something.

From what R. Aaron calls "God's point of view," however, these mind-states aren't really there at all. For R. Aaron, like his teacher Rabbi Schneur Zalman of Liady, the founder of Chabad Hasidism, every thing that we think of as existing is actually "absolute nothing and emptiness," and all that actually exists is what seems to be absolute emptiness, *ayin*: God. As in the J.D. Salinger short story "Teddy," this moment is God reading God. It is emptiness reading emptiness: a myriad of causes and conditions, none of them independent from anything else, empty phenomena rolling on.

Admittedly, these are only metaphysical propositions. But they do align with certain experiences of the selfless, the deathless, that often arise when the ordinary boundaries of consciousness are shifted. Who knows what those experiences really are—but at least the mere metaphysics and the mere empiricism align with one another.

Both perspectives, too, may be theistic or non-theistic. The theistic *yesh* is the God to whom I cry; the theistic *ayin* is the God which cries through me. The non-theistic *yesh* comprises all my stuff, my gender, my sexuality, my life; the non-theistic *ayin* sees that all this stuff is a set of empty phenomena, rolling on, with no one guiding the boat.

And together with each attitude is a kind of action. Psychologically, what might be called *yesh*-work deals with phenomena as they arise: therapy and psychoanalysis; *cheshbon hanefesh*, which literally means 'accounting of the soul,'; non-violent communication; somatic practices. Each of these can be helpful in working with the stuff of our lives. What might be called *ayin*-work drops the phenomena and experiences the pain as an apparent ripple in Emptiness. This is more akin to the predominant disposition of the gate of tears: letting-be, allowing, dropping, coexisting, not changing. A kind of *Shabbat* of the mind.

It is not that one perspective is right and the other is wrong. In this view, both the ripples and the non-ripples are truthful descriptions of what is going on. From our own humanistic perspectives, it hardly seems worth the bother for God to disguise Herself as us, only for us to drop the disguise and melt. Fortunately, that seems impossible anyway. It does seem worthwhile to occasionally experience one's life from a perspective other than that of the self. Insight, bliss, a taste of the sacred—perhaps not essential, but worthwhile.

To see from God's point of view is not meant to be a permanent condition for a second reason: there is a world to heal. The compassion that flows naturally from enlightenment distinguishes it from mere ecstasy, and invites us to engage with the world. That engagement, in turn, requires a sort of *tzimtzum* on the personal level, a contraction back into finitude, a return to caring. We might suppose that, if suffering does not really exist, then the enlightened one would simply surrender to the Allness of God, inherent in cancer wards just as much as in verdant fields. But somehow it is not so.

Somehow, and this seems miraculous, the true unity includes both God's point of view and our own points of view, and as a consequence cares about our transitory pain. At moments of enlightenment, all is transcended and included in the One. Sadness does not disappear; it is included in a serene and compassionate embrace.

There is, thus, reality, and unreality, to tears. Which perspective is real, and which unreal? That, too, is a matter of perspective.

The Strange Accessibility of Love

To be religious about one's tears is to talk about love.

The projection of human love onto the screen of the Absolute is to imagine a love at once akin to and radically different from that of human relationship. If we take earthly love for granted, it may disappear. If we neglect our loved ones, and do not express our own love in words and actions, they may cease to love us. Likewise, if we smother one another with affection, and do not provide room for independence and growth—in this case, too, love can vanish.

The Jewish path projects these aspects of human love onto the Divine. We tend to our Beloved, in words and in actions. And most Jewish mystics are careful not to allow their love of God to replace their engagement with the world. Even at the heights of ecstasy, they know they are to return to the marketplace, to their families, to the work of pursuing justice. And even as they experience love of the Divine as they understand it, that love is shaped by the human world and its interactions. They give voice to longing, consummation, and renewed longing in the realm of the sacred because they have known it in the realm of the worldly.

Like other Western theisms, the Jewish path projects these aspects of human love onto the Divine. On the one hand, Jewish mystics write rapturous love poems to the One, giving voice to the longing, the consummation, and the longing anew. On the other hand, Jewish contemplatives insist that the love of God must not occlude human being's responsibilities toward one another. Even at their monistic, panentheistic extremes, Jewish mystics demand a kind of religious polyamory: love of God and of people, of heaven and of earth. Of course, their concomitant insistence that all is one renders the "poly" into "pan."

Trust

It is a strange thing—that love is so accessible, even to one alone, and even throughout the inevitable impermanence of change, growth, loss, and death. Remarkably, there is a human capacity to experience love undifferentiated and unparticularized, its object the eternal You. Religious people call this undifferentiated love the Love of God. And when I am broken, it is almost impossible to withstand tears at its encounter. *Trust*

Hinei el yeshuati, evtach v'lo efchad—Behold, God is my salvation, I will trust and not fear. These words from the Book of Psalms are recited as part of the Havdalah service, which separates the holy time of Shabbat from the ordinary time of the rest of the week. Moving from a time of constructed sanctuary, abiding in the spaciousness of the *shechinah*, into a time of necessary constriction into our ego-selves, it is natural to fear. In the non-linear moment, all is well. But in the world of time, things require our attention. We are dissatisfied, working to improve things, and thus inevitably subject to the first and second Noble Truths—that craving brings suffering.

So the liturgy says not to be afraid. I read it not as promising that pain will be kept at bay, since that is impossible, but rather that God will be with you wherever you are, even in the pain; that there will remain accessible a reservoir of unconditional love that is either Divine or, more remarkably, a natural capacity of the human heart. The trust in this faculty of mind (or, if you prefer, grace of God) is a kind of salvation.

This is always here. (*Hinei* means "behold" but also "Here.") This path is about what always is and what sometimes is.

That being said, it is probably easier to experience God in a hospital bed than in a conference room.

Ecclesiastes

The book of Kohelet—Ecclesiastes—is often regarded as pessimistic. "All is vanity!" says Kohelet, the preacher, traditionally identified with King Solomon. Kohelet has sought, and attained, riches, wisdom, love—everything we might wish for. And yet he declares them all vanity.

"Vanity," though, is a poor translation of the Hebrew word *hevel*. *Hevel* has as its root the expiration of air. A better rendition of it would be transitory, passing, empty. All is transitory, Kohelet is saying. Nothing lasts forever.

That said, it *is* vanity to suppose that ourselves or our achievements have lasting memory. "I am Ozymandias," boasts an inscription near a set of Egyptian ruins, in Shelley's poem. "Look on my works, ye mighty, and despair." The Pharoah's proclamation is meant as a boast, but takes on an unintended irony, because, as Shelley writes, "nothing beside remains." Ozymandias wanted the mighty to despair at his power; instead they despair at his powerlessness. All we create is *hevel*.

But this supposed pessimism is only one side of the story. Kohelet does propose an alternative:

> Emptiness of emptiness, says Kohelet; emptiness of emptiness; everything is empty.
> Of what profit to man is all the labor that he does under the sun?
> A generation comes, a generation goes. But the Earth endures forever.

The sun comes and shines, and rushes to another place, and shines there.

The wind blows south, and turns to the north, and turns, and turns in its turning, and on its turning path it returns again.

All the rivers run to the sea—but the sea is never full. To the place from whence the rivers ran, they will return to run again.

Cyclical time is the alternative. In our linear minds, things have permanence, and processes lead to conclusions. The rivers run to the sea, the sea should eventually become full. We get disappointed when this does not happen, when things do not last.

But in the cyclical aspect of time, nothing is permanent, and no process is ever concluded. The ecological cycle of rivers and winds; the generations coming and going. As long as we attach ourselves to linear time, we will be disappointed. When it is possible to know intuitively that to every thing there is a season, and that no achievements are lasting, then a deeper happiness is possible. Kohelet becomes the recipe for liberation.

Likewise, today some earth-based communities chant: "We all come from the goddess / And to Her, we shall return / Like a drop of rain / Flowing to the ocean." This is not despair, but celebration—or at least acquiescence. Consider some of Kohelet's ostensibly despairing pronouncements in this light:

There are righteous ones who are given what the evil deserve, and evil ones who are given what the righteous deserve. I said, this too is *hevel*.

Everything comes to everyone: one end to the righteous and to the wicked; to the good and pure and to the impure; to the pious and the impious.

The good man is the same as the sinner.

Is this not true? Of course it is the case that evil exists and that it seems to go unpunished. Human evil—the Holocaust, the Middle Passage. Natural evil—children with cancer. Or my personal pain, my own losses, my own mortality. Accidents. From a linear perspective, it is good to combat evil with all that we've got. But it will not necessarily result in justice. *Hevel*—the relative silence of the tides.

And we are all dying, and will all soon die. But this is realism, not pessimism; instead of saying goodbye to life, as the pop song goes, say hello. *Memento Mori.* Remember death to savor life as it passes. Recognize that sensual pleasures are fleeting, and will be followed by suffering. The same mistakes will be made over and over again.

The gate of tears opens when the locks of expectation are released. It's not that temporary things are valueless; they are simply *hevel.* They are transitory, vaporous. Kohelet's river-consciousness is not one of despair. Being is unfolding. The birds are not despairing because they will soon be dead. They are singing.

A Hasidic Mystery Tale

A Hasidic story about joy in sadness:

There was once a hasid who could not meet his debts and, as

was the practice at the time, was thrown into jail. This hasid was very pious, and strove to keep all of the *mitzvot* he could while in jail. But the chamber-pot that he and his cellmates used was kept in the jail cell itself. This meant that he was forbidden to put on *tefillin*, one of the holiest and most important commandments of all.

The hasid became extremely sad because he could not put on *tefillin*. It may help us to understand his sadness if we know that *tefillin* is described as the wedding ring between the Jew and God: when it is wrapped around the finger, the words of betrothal are uttered. So not only was the hasid cut off from his earthly wife and family, but now he was also bereft of his heavenly betrothed as well. He was utterly alone.

The hasid's rebbe came to visit him in jail, and the hasid poured out his heart in front of him.

"And why aren't you putting on *tefillin*?" the rebbe asked.

The hasid, sure that the rebbe knew the answer, nonetheless replied that it was forbidden to put on *tefillin* in a place where there was exposed human waste.

"So this is a great joy!" said the rebbe. "You should be dancing before *Hashem* that you have this opportunity to fulfill this mitzvah of not putting on *tefillin*! Most of us never have the chance."

The hasid immediately became filled with great joy.

The story does not end there, however. The hasid, recognizing that indeed, the prohibition regarding *tefillin* was indeed a mitzvah which not every Jew had the chance to fulfill, was filled with elation at this new and precious way of serving God. In fact, he became so filled with joy that he followed the rebbe's instructions and started dancing for God. His joyfulness was infectious. Soon his cellmates were dancing and singing and rejoicing at the Divine Presence.

One guard asked another why all the Jews were celebrating.

"I don't know, but it has something to do with the chamber-pot," the other guard replied.

"Well, I'll show them!" the first guard said. And he removed the chamber-pot from the cell!

The Tears that Surpass Idolatry

Through the gate of tears, the invitation is to cast aside the ascriptions of the word "God" to positive mindstates, to subjective feelings of closeness, or to any qualities, positive or negative, with which we may prefer to associate the Divine. Thus the gate invites the dropping of concepts and dogmas regarding the absolute.

What many of us mean when we say "God" is really just the projection of a feeling. I feel connected, or loved, and I say that means God is here. Many times, the religious experience is the externalization of a private, subjective feeling. But if "God" is "how the world feels when I am happy," does that mean that God is absent when I am sad? Or, when I have contracted back from ecstasy into whatever comes next (the laundry, the loneliness, the dissatisfaction), do I have the courage to affirm that this, too, is God?

To suppose that God is only in the fire of ecstasy—or only on the *kol d'mamah dakah*, the silent and thin voice that follows it—is to limit the limitless. It is to love some of experience, but not all of it.

The error of idolatry is not so much that an idol is made, but that the idol alone is thought to be a god. What about the stone that was discarded?

When God Kvetches

I often don't seem very 'spiritual' to friends, colleagues, Twitter followers, or myself. This is helpful at parties (spiritual people are often incredibly annoying) but more importantly, I grow more spiritually awake when I don't want to seem that way.

Example: When it's cold and gray and raining a mix of water and snow, I kvetch. A friend replies, in spiritual-speak, that "Oh, but rain is so important—this is God manifesting as rain!"

God, that is irritating.

Here's how I would reply if I weren't afraid of seeming pedantic. Yes, this is God as rain. But this is also God as my conditioned mind responding to bad weather. It, too, is part of the web. So can I accept both the weather and the mind's reaction to it? Can I relax and not pretend to be all 'spiritual,' instead making peace with the grumpiness? Accepting the small mind is the only way not to make a big deal out of it.

When this works, something quite delightful happens. A warm peace comes over me, and a little smile appears. The weather is bad, and the weather is God. I kvetch about the weather, and I love the kvetch, because it too is part of Indra's Net, part of the Matrix, part of God.

Kvetch all you want—that is my kind of liberation!

And obviously, I'm not just talking about the weather.

The Awareness of a Leaf

How can one gain the awareness of a leaf?

I mean more than 'being aware of a leaf.' To be sure, in a quiet mind, a leaf's veins, surfaces, and colors arrest the eye. Contemplative practice yield an extraordinary sight of the ordinary.

But I also mean: How can one approximate the leaf's own awareness, unconscious, automatic, and immediate? This is not awareness in the usual sense, of course; the leaf is not thinking. I mean it in way that rocks "know" the laws of the universe and vast reaches of outer space "know" the forces acting upon them. Pure causality, without consciousness. The way the atoms in your eye, as you read these words, were once part of a star.

Organizing all this matter and energy are the laws of physics, the laws of nature. This kind of knowing does not depend upon thought or feeling. Is it possible to perceive it, or at least imagine it, as the moments tick by? Does it not provide a counterpoint to the in-breaths and out-breaths of emotion? Here is a dissolving of tears into water.

No Sides

The poet says: When I look into my beloved's eyes, God sees Godself. This is untenable as theology or philosophy. It is only the profound sense of being at home.

The warrior says: God is on our side. But God is the condition in which there are no sides. Not even an inside or an outside.

Undissolved differentiation still persists. Better not to cross the street without looking, even as a mystic. As the *hadith* quotes Prophet Muhammad as saying, trust in Allah, but tie up your camel. Also better not to allow cruelty, injustice, privilege to increase.

And there is still ordinary pain, and the adaptive impulse to get rid of it. Even saying "this is part of God's plan" is also an attempt to get rid of it. Allow, allow, allow.

There are no sides, no plan. There is what there is.

Rabbi Nachman of Bratzlav

Rabbi Nachman of Bratzlav is the great Jewish prophet of sadness. This is so even though one of his most beloved aphorisms is *mitzvah gedolah liyhot b'simcha tamid*, that it is a great commandment to be happy always.

But we know from Rabbi Nachman's writings that he was not a man always in joy, at least not in the conventional sense. His life was one of struggles, both emotional and physical, and his religious outlook was one which valued the process of struggling much more than the result of it. Most famously, Rabbi Nachman made an extremely arduous, nearly fatal pilgrimage to the Land of Israel, but once he got there, he was ready to go back. It was the struggle of making the trip that was important.

We also have many stories of the "tormented master," as Arthur Green labeled him, seemingly in states of mania or depression, often in such pain that he becomes unable to lead his Hasidim, and often in such heightened emotional states that, he says, just a small movement of a finger contains all the intensity of ecstatic prayer. Rabbi Nachman practiced a new method of *hitbodedut*, an emotionally visceral outpouring of the soul, alone before God. Even today, it is possible to hear Nachman's followers, late at night, in the woods outside Tsfat or Jerusalem, crying and pleading in this way.

It is perhaps surprising that Breslov Hasidism (the faithful pronounce it "Breslov," the scholars "Bratzlav") continues to thrive today, despite the fact that the Rebbe has been dead for two hundred years and no successor was ever named. There are ever-increasing pilgrimages to Rabbi Nachman's grave, divergent sects of devotees, and, of course, video and audio streaming online.

Because of Rabbi Nachman's ethos of struggle, his God-language is often highly dualistic. Many Breslov prayers are paeans to an absent God, begging Him to come closer. While the concept of *devekut* (cleaving to God) is present in Rabbi Nachman's teachings, it is not seen as a state we always enjoy, all of the time. It comes and goes. Sometimes the One seems to be in eclipse.

Spirituality can be a trap. *You're nothing but God, you know, so why do you feel so bad?* The gate of tears is a potential trap, too: *If you still feel lousy, you must not be doing it right; come on, then, love the sadness.*

No, sometimes it is inauthentic not to want.

To allow the wanting—and to render it sacred. Rabbi Nachman calls up our pain, demands the confrontation of our brokenness, and promises its expiation only after arduous personal effort.

Thus the paradox: that the prophet of joy is a man who cried out nightly to God. That the preacher of sadness taught us always to be joyful. Some understand these teachings to mean that one must descend in order to ascend, to fall into sadness in order later to emerge into joy. And it is true that when catharsis is achieved after a long period of struggle, the release is sweet.

But Breslov's greatest value may lie at the other pole of consciousness, when the path of holy suffering is the only tether to hope. The descent happens with or without intention, and Rabbi Nachman cries with the courage to be broken.

Yielding to Struggling

More from Rabbi Nachman:

> In general, one must try with all one's might to be joyful
> always. For it is human nature to be drawn to bitterness
> and sadness because of the wounds one has suffered—and
> every person is full of troubles. So one must force oneself,
> with a great effort, to be happy always....
>
> Now, it is also true that a broken heart is very good—but
> only at certain times. So, it is wise to set an hour each day
> to break one's heart and talk to God, as we do. But the rest
> of the day, one must be in joy.

There is something tragic in this text from *Likutei Moharan* (II,
24; my translation): the notion that people are inclined toward
sadness, and that it requires a great effort to be otherwise. Ahead
of his time, Rabbi Nachman prescribed a therapeutic hour of
brokenheartedness—he refers here to *hitbodedut*, the practice of
secluding oneself and talking, crying, and free-associating to
God in solitude. He does this because otherwise, sadness might
take over the rest of the day as well. For him, happiness requires
force.

Reb Nachman is careful to distinguish a broken heart from
depression. In another collection of his oral teachings, *Sichot
HaRan*, he says that depression is evil, hated by God, and more
akin to anger than sadness. "It is like a complaint against God
for not fulfilling one's wishes" (*Sichot HaRan* 42). A broken
heart, however, "is very dear and precious to God... one with a

broken heart is like a child pleading before his father. He is like a baby crying and complaining because his father is far away."

This distinction between the transitory, healthy oscillation of feelings on the one hand, and a condition of depression on the other, is quite prescient, given that it was made in approximately 1805. For Rabbi Nachman, the broken heart is a pure sadness motivated by love. It is not a complaint that we haven't gotten what we wanted; it's an expression of the existential condition of yearning. And ultimately, "After heartbreak comes joy," Rabbi Nachman says. "Being happy later on is a true sign of having a broken heart." (Sichot HaRan 45) Rabbi Nachman ennobles sadness like no one in the Jewish tradition, before or since. For better or for worse. And it seems that for Rabbi Nachman, the struggle is at least as valuable as its consummation.

Consider Rabbi Nachman's pilgrimage to the Land of Israel. In the early nineteenth century, such a path was fraught with peril, and there were many occasions on which the great rebbe almost died. Yet when he reached the Promised Land, he was immediately ready to go back. His disciples had to convince him to stay longer and visit the holy sites and communities. For Rabbi Nachman, it was the journey—not the destination—that was significant.

Yet struggle is not necessarily the opposite of surrender. Rabbi Nachman urges a surrender to the struggle: giving up the desire not to have to struggle. Struggle with your sadness, he says, struggle with your soul, struggle with your body and its urges. The point is not to rid oneself of struggle, but to accept it as a condition of being human. We are not meant to prevail. We must make room in the soul for an existential condition of lack.

Having said that, I admit that this path is not my own. I

struggled for many years: with my identity, my sexuality, my Judaism, my doubts about Judaism, my fit or mis-fit with conventional modes of living, my family, my career, my ambition. At this point, I find it more skillful to accept that which others would struggle against. It is why Rabbi Nachman is an inspiration, but not my teacher.

Rabbi Nachman's gateway is to love the pain that comes from struggle. If you are struggling for a holy purpose (and caring for others, providing for them, is certainly one), then the pain you experience along the way is holy.

"Woe is us!" says Rabbi Nachman. "The world is full of light and mysteries both wonderful and awesome, but our tiny little hand shades our eyes and prevents them from seeing."

Guilt

As I have said, the gate of tears is not the predominant approach to sadness in either mainstream or mystical Judaism. In Hasidism, for example, sadness is regarded with great mistrust and hostility. For example, the Baal Shem Tov says at one point that "sorrow prevents us from carrying out our task of worshiping the Creator."

My interest here is not to harmonize such teachings with my own; I would rather investigate the discord. But here is the fuller passage from the Baal Shem Tov:

Sometimes our evil inclination tries to lead us astray by telling us that something we have done is a grave sin, when it is really just a minor infraction or perhaps no sin at all. It does this in order to make us sorrowful, for sorrow prevents us from carrying out our task of worshiping the Creator.

In other words, what the Baal Shem Tov is talking about is not sadness, but guilt. Remember, he was speaking to an audience that was taught to see themselves as sinful. As we know from our own day, the sense of one's inadequacy, one's own sinfulness, can be the predominant modality of religious life.

Even for those of us who are not religious in this way, we all know the Jewish emphasis on guilt, right?

Sometimes it's useful to be aware of feeling guilty, like the clear seeing of where we have fallen short. All of us have said things we wish we had not said, or done, and many of us are haunted in our dreams by the friends and lovers we drove away. What is our response? Often, I replay the misplaced words or thoughtless deed over and over again. The state of discomfort with what I have said or done is so great that it is actually easier to masochistically replay the scene than to sit still with the sense of having made a mistake. I wrack myself with guilt precisely because I cannot sit with the guilt.

So maybe the consciousness of today's guilt-ridden sinners, or yesterday's guilt-ridden pious Jews, is not so incomprehensible. And if so, the Baal Shem Tov's warning is a welcome one. Guilt can lead to a sense of inadequacy that can be debilitating. Sometimes it is useful, but sometimes it comes from the "evil inclination." Sometimes it is holy to let it go.

The Root

Among the early Hasidic masters, devotional prayer was a paramount spiritual exercise. Consequently, what to do about distraction was of crucial importance—as it is for meditators as well, of course. The intention may be to cultivate states of ecstasy, but the mind wanders off to more mundane matters.

The Baal Shem Tov, the founder of Hasidism, proposed an innovative method for dealing with distraction. At the time, most rabbis advised their followers to banish any trace of the distracting thought; if you're fantasizing about a beautiful body, imagine it decomposing. But the Baal Shem Tov held that such thoughts could be "brought near to God." (Keter Shem Tov § 171) If you are thinking of a beautiful body, take its beauty to its root: supernal beauty, the quality of beauty. If you are thinking of financial issues, take that thought to its root: perhaps, the desire to support your family, or fear, or a need for help.

Likewise, in the very different key of American Buddhism, Joseph Goldstein notes in *The Experience of Insight* that it is possible to have compassion even for dark emotions that arise during meditation. Suppose I'm feeling greed, for example. Okay. Well, that greed is a psychological mechanism that my mind has developed to try to ensure that I have enough: enough love, enough security, whatever. Ultimately, these 'dark' thoughts also want what's best for us—even if they are deeply confused. It's not that it's good to feel greedy, or envious, or terrified, but it is possible to see through them.

This practice helps me time and time again, when I'm caught

in longing, anger, or sadness. I try to take the feeling to its root. What is it that I'm wanting, right now, if taken to its logical conclusion? Usually, it's love, safety, security. Sometimes it's power, but that, too, is really a desire to feel secure, safe, and important. Or suppose there's a longing for a connection with another person; you can experience, right in the moment, the love or consummation or pleasure you imagine with that person. Use your imagination; call up what it might be like to have that experience of nearness and intimacy.

Take the poison to its root, and it resolves into something easier to be near. Or perhaps that which is already nearer to you than the self that is afraid of it.

It is Hard to Be Lonely in a Waterfall

I'm twenty years old and sitting in a waterfall near Bulls Bridge, Connecticut. It's a summer afternoon; the sun is shining and the water is pounding down on my body. That morning, I had been reading Fritjof Capra's *The Tao of Physics*, which notes parallels between Buddhist and Hindu teachings on the nature of reality and some interpretations of contemporary physics. I was that kind of twenty-year-old.

Sitting under the waterfall, I suddenly felt indistinguishable from it. What was the difference between the water and me? Only information; only the laws of physics organizing this part of reality into Me, and that other part into Waterfall. I felt like I got it, and I felt connected.

Later, I learned that one of the fundamental teachings of the Kabbalah is that the world is created with language. Not just in the Biblical sense ("And God Said…") but ontologically as well: the *Sefer Yetzirah* (Book of Creation) posits that the universe was formed by means of Hebrew letters. Because this teaching reifies the Hebrew alphabet (a product of human history), and because it is tied to the mythological Genesis story, it is easy to disregard these myths. But Kabbalah, together with alchemy, was a forerunner of modern chemistry. Its theory of language was not a form of poetry as much as of science. The Kabbalists understood letters much as we understand the periodic table: as the constituent elements of existence. Kabbalistically speaking, letters are both the vocabulary and the grammar of the world.

Now we understand that the universe is constructed not by letters, but by those same laws and bits of information that I had been reading about. On the macro level, a tree exists because the genetic material in its DNA has organized the matter and energy received from soil, water, and light into the form of a tree. On the micro level, the matter is organized into molecules, and the molecules into atoms, according to a few basic principles, which together interact in an uncountable number of ways; the matter and energy interact the way they do because of basic principles which ultimately reduce down to a handful of basic laws (gravity, weak and strong subatomic forces, electromagnetism). For now.

I'm not suggesting that the Kabbalists intuited post-Newtonian physics. But it can be of use to translate physics back into the poetic language of myth.

Why does this matter, apart from its intellectual interest? Because it becomes harder to remain lonely in a waterfall.

Truth

When the truth of experience is granted, its often minor-key melody enshrouds us like a blanket of memory.

The mind rushes to distract or denigrate, but I think of Psalm 145's audacious promise that "God is near to all who call upon God, to all who call upon God in truth." In one sense, the second half of the line seems like a hedge. In another sense, however, the second half is a definition: that to be spiritually authentic is to be truthful.

If the truth of our experience is modulated in keys of sadness, then that is our truth. If the truth of our being is that of joy, or achievement, or self-expression, then that is our truth. Either way, to authentically be religious (to "call upon God"), requires truthfulness rather than deceit.

Hoping to somehow evade, banish, or crush sadness is false consciousness. So is glorifying, dramatizing, or otherwise justifying it. What is actually happening? This is the religious question. When whatever is happening is accepted, it can then perhaps be loved. When the gate of tears is opened truthfully, the world's beauty opens up within it. Each screech of a taxicab's brakes is like the fourfold song of the universe.

Whatever God is, it must be closely related to truth.

The Embrace

Would you judge, repress, banish, justify, or apologize for a musical note?

Put another way, this is the invitation, perhaps unwelcome: to act with hospitality toward the unwanted houseguests of the heart, make room for them, surrender. They are not anomalies, distractions from what is important. They are not flaws in the system. They are a feature, not a bug.

The only way out is through; it is not possible to deny, avoid, or repress one's way to freedom. The fears, the cracks, the empty spaces: the only way out is through. Through the gateless gate which is never shut.

It is ordinary to be amazed at the wondrous—but wondrous to be amazed at the ordinary. And taken to its root, the ordinary is what has always been here: only the is-ness of is, the simple freedom of relinquishment into truth.

What we talk about when we talk about God in this way is the possibility of yielding to, merging with the causes and conditions, the empty phenomena that make up the fullness of experience. There are no inner or outer limits to this emptiness, this freedom; there is no place it is not. We are only unhappy when we want to be somewhere else.

Which, conveniently, we can never be.

Leave the burden to God. Meaning, set it down; release it from your grasp. Ajahn Sucitto, another British-born Thai monk who says, "right now, it's like that," tells a short parable. He says that we are all like a donkey pulling a cart, impelled by the desire for the carrot dangling a few inches from its face. Some carrots are easy to mock—those superficial desires for trinkets and validations. But some are profound: love, success, freedom from fear and want. Yet as delightful as the carrot may seem, what the donkey cannot know is that what it really wants is to rest, to set down the burden.

The donkey cannot know it, but we can begin to feel it, with each instant of surrendering, resting, *Shabbat*. It is not only a release. It is an embrace, too, that contains a certain secret, which rests beyond the reasons for love.

The Gate of Tears

Acknowledgments

Thanks to Rabbi Jacob Staub and Rev. Jakob Hero, for their help and support in the wake of my mother's illness, and to my mother's many friends in New York and Tampa who were so loving and so generous. Thanks to teachers whose wisdom appears in this book, including Shoshana Cooper, Lama Surya Das, Rabbi Arthur Green, Sylvia Boorstein, Sharon Salzberg, Shinzen Young, Ajahn Sucitto, Eliezer Sobel, Rabbi David Cooper, Andrew Ramer, Michael Cohen, and Rabbi Zalman Schachter-Shalomi, of blessed memory. Thanks to my co-teachers, Beth Resnick, Rabbi Naomi Hyman, Rabbi Shir Yaakov Feit, Rabbi David Ingber, Rabbi Jill Hammer, Shoshana Jedwab, Kenneth Folk, and Leigh Brasington. Thanks to Larry Yudelson, Josh Baran, Dan Harris, Adam Segulah Sher, Eden Pearlstein, Ethan Sobel, and the Jewish Book Council. Thanks to circles of friendship in the Radical Faerie, Burning Man, American Buddhist, Dharma Punx, and Alt-Jewish communities. Thank to inspiring colleagues at The Daily Beast and the Forward. Thanks to my mother and my father, both of blessed memory; to Maia, Nancy, and Henry; and to Paul, for patience and joy.

The Gate of Tears

Bibliography and Works Cited

Sylvia Boorstein, *Happiness is an Inside Job* (Ballantine, 2008)

—. *That's Funny, You Don't Look Buddhist* (HarperOne, 1998)

Sylvia Boorstein, Norman Fischer, and Tsoknyi Rinpoche, *Solid Ground: Buddhist Wisdom for Difficult Times* (Parallax, 2011)

Tara Brach, *Radical Acceptance: Embracing Your Life with the Heart of a Buddha* (Bantam, 2003)

Pema Chödrön, *When Things Fall Apart* (Shambhala, 2000)

—, *Comfortable with Uncertainty* (Shambhala, 2003)

—, *Fail, Fail Again, Fail Better* (Sounds True, 2015)

Leonard Cohen, *Book of Longing* (Ecco, 2007 ed.)

Louis Dupré, *The Other Dimension* (Seabury, 1979)

Barbara Ehrenreich, *Bright-Sided* (Picador, 2010)

Mark Epstein, *Going to Pieces without Falling Apart* (Broadway, 1999)

Alina N. Feld, *Melancholy and the Otherness of God* (Lexington, 2011)

David Feldman & Lee Daniel Kravetz, *Supersurvivors: The Surprising Link Between Suffering and Success* (HarperWave, 2014)

Frederick Franck, *Zen of Seeing* (Vintage, 1973)

Allen Ginsberg, *Collected Poems 1947-1997* (Harper Perennial 2007)

Joseph Goldstein, *The Experience of Insight* (Shambhala, 1987 ed.)

Niles Goldstein, *Lost Souls: Finding Hope in the Heart of Darkness* (Harmony/Bell Tower, 2002)

Daniel Goleman, *Emotional Intelligence* (Bantam, 2005 ed.)

Arthur Green, *Tormented Master: The Life and Spiritual Quest of Rabbi Nachman of Bratzlav* (Jewish Lights, 1992 ed.)`

Miriam Greenspan, *Healing Through the Dark Emotions* (Shambhala, 2003)

Judith Halberstam, *The Queer Art of Failure* (Duke, 2011)

Joan Halifax, *Being with Dying* (Shambhala, 2009 ed.)

Dan Harris, *10% Happier* (It Books, 2014)

Russ Harris, *The Happiness Trap* (Shambhala, 2008)

Allan Horwitz & Jerome Wakefield, *The Loss of Sadness* (Oxford, 2007)

Langston Hughes, *The Collected Poems of Langston Hughes*, ed. by Arnold Rampersad (Vintage, 1995)

Ikkyu, trans. by Stephen Berg, *Crow with No Mouth* (Copper Canyon,

2000)

David Karp, *Speaking of Sadness* (Oxford, 1997)

Byron Katie, *Loving What Is* (Three Rivers, 2003 ed.)

Jack Kornfield, *After the Ecstasy, the Laundry* (Bantam, 2001)

Søren Kierkegaard, trans. by A.S. Aldworth & W.S. Ferrie, Gospel of Sufferings (James Clarke, 2015 ed.)

Harold Kushner, *When Bad Things Happen to Good People* (Anchor, 2004 ed.)

C.S. Lewis, *A Grief Observed* (HarperOne, 2015 ed.)

Sherri Mandell, *The Blessing of a Broken Heart* (Toby Press, 2003)

Philip Martin, *The Zen Path through Depression* (Harper, 2000).

Jay Michaelson, *Everything is God: The Radical Path of Nondual Judaism* (Shambhala/Trumpeter, 2009)

—*Evolving Dharma: Meditation, Buddhism, and the Next Generation of Enlightenment* (North Atlantic, 2013)

Rabbi Nathan of Nemirov, trans. by Aryeh Kaplan, *Rabbi Nachman's Wisdom*, (Breslov Research Institute, 1973)

Rainer Maria Rilke, trans. by Anita Barrows & Joanna Macy, *Rilke's Book of Hours* (Riverhead, 1996)

—trans. by Robert Bly, *Selected Poems of Rainer Maria Rilke* (Harper & Row, 1981)

Ryokan, trans. by John Stevens, *One Robe, One Bowl: The Zen Poetry of Ryokan* (Weatherhill, 1977)

Sharon Salzberg, *Faith* (Riverhead, 2003)

Friedrich Schleiermacher, trans. by Richard Crouter, *On Religion: Lectures to its Cultured Despisers* (Cambridge University Press, 1996)

Philip Simmons, *Learning to Fall: The Blessings of an Imperfect Life* (Bantam, 2000)

Andrew Solomon, *The Noonday Demon* (Scribner, 2002)

Zalman Sorotzkin, *Insights in the Torah, Volume 1* (Artscroll 1991)

William Styron, *Darkness Visible* (Cape, 1991)

Ajahn Sucitto, "Donkeys and Carrots," dharmaseed.org/teacher/9/talk/14862/

Surya Das, *Letting Go of the Person You Used to Be* (Harmony, 2004)

John Tarrant, *The Light Inside the Dark* (HarperCollins, 1998)

Elie Wiesel, *Four Hasidic Masters and their Struggle Against Melancholy* (Notre Dame, 1978)

Rabbi Dr. Jay Michaelson is the author of six books, most recently *Evolving Dharma: Meditation, Buddhism and the Next Generation of Enlightenment* (North Atlantic, 2013). He is a columnist for *The Daily Beast* and *Forward*, and has written over three hundred articles, primarily on intersections of religion, sexuality, spirituality, and law. As an LGBT activist, he founded two Jewish LGBT organizations, wrote the bestselling book *God vs. Gay? The Religious Case for Equality* (Beacon, 2013), and now co-directs the *Quorum: Global LGBT Voices* project, connecting Western audiences with LGBT leaders from the Global South. He appears often on NPR, CNN, MSNBC, and similar venues talking about these subjects.

In his other life as a meditation, Dharma, and Jewish teacher/scholar, Jay has taught at Omega, Elat Chayyim, Burning Man, Dharma Punx, New York Insight, Kripalu, and about one hundred synagogues and Jewish institutions across the country. In the academy, Dr. Michaelson is currently an Affiliated Assistant Professor at Chicago Theological Seminary, and has held teaching positions at Yale University, Boston University Law School, and Harvard Divinity School. He holds a PhD in Jewish Thought from Hebrew University of Jerusalem, a JD from Yale Law School, an MFA from Sarah Lawrence, a BA from Columbia, and non-denominational rabbinic ordination.

CPSIA information can be obtained
at www.ICGtesting.com
Printed in the USA
FFOW03n2007161117
43593206-42394FF